CW00672924

Painted Wings

ROBIN SMITH

First published 2016
Second edition printed 2017

Design by Papermouse

ISBN: 978-1-5262-0170-6

Acknowledgements

The Author would like to thank the following for their help and co operation in the production of this book.
I wish to thank Captain Darryl Elliott, Captain Nick Stein and Dr Ian Campbell for their expert proof reading. Squadron Ldr Clive Rowley (former Commanding Officer of the Battle of Britain Memorial Flight), for writing the very much appreciated Foreword. Louise and Neil at Papermouse, drawing on their experience and knowledge to design the final book presentation. They worked tirelessly to ensure the meeting of an important deadline for completion. I would also like to mention of all the clients who purchased my paintings, and allowed their names to be mentioned in the book alongside the images of their paintings, too numerous to name individually in my acknowledgments. Finally I would like to thank my wife Carol who kept me sane, feeding me tea and the odd can of beer. I not only couldn't have done it without her….I wouldn't have wanted to do it without her.

Contents In Alphabetical Order Of Manufacturer

Dedicated to my wife Carol
and my daughter Hayley.

Foreword

Squadron Leader Clive Rowley MBE RAF (Retd)
(Former Officer Commanding the RAF Battle of Britain Memorial Flight and RAF fighter pilot)

I have known Robin Smith for some 20 years, since I first started flying with the RAF Battle of Britain Memorial Flight (BBMF), and during that time I have taken a close interest in his aviation paintings. Indeed, when I was on the ground at air shows where I knew that he would have a tent exhibiting and selling his paintings, I would always seek it out to chat to Robin and his lovely wife, Carol, and to see his latest masterpieces. Sometimes he would have a work-in-progress painting on an easel, which he might actually be working on, and I could watch the painting evolve to the finished version and marvel at his attention to detail and his subtle changes to the composition.

I am sure that the things that Robin has done in his life, which he tells of in the short autobiography in this book, have equipped him in an almost unique way to be able to paint aviation subjects. It will probably come as no surprise that he has held a life-long interest in aircraft and aviation, which will perhaps be shared by many who choose to own this book. As a result, he has built up expert knowledge of his subjects; he is an aviation historian as well as an aviation artist. Earlier in his life he worked as a draughtsman for Rolls Royce, which must have taught him technical skills important to an artist. In addition, he has been a private pilot since 1968 (which, incidentally, is the same year that I gained my Private Pilot's Licence, at the age of 17 and before I could drive a car), experience which provides him with a pilot's perspective of his subject aircraft, especially in the air. His time as a sailor in the Royal Navy will also have added to his appreciation of skies and weather. Pilots and sailors share a professional interest in the sky and the weather it produces; they are sometimes privileged to see skies that ordinary people do not see, or perhaps simply do not notice.

Skies, the mood of the weather, the lighting and the colouring that these conditions produce are important in aviation paintings, perhaps especially to a pilot like me. The sunsets, sunrises, mist, reflections in water or the state of the sea in Robin's paintings add hugely to the composition and the atmosphere. The dark, threatening sky and the rainbow in his 'Bombing up Yorker', a copy of which hung in the BBMF headquarters at RAF Coningsby for all of my time with the Flight, is a good example.

You will have gathered by now that I am a great fan of Robin's paintings and I actually own two limited-edition prints of his work. 'At the Going Down of the Sun' is his beautiful, cleverly titled painting of the BBMF Lancaster with a Hurricane and a Spitfire returning to Coningsby from the south, passing the Wash, as the sun sets on the day's flying. I've been there in that formation doing just that and I've been in the privileged position of seeing the bomber and the other fighter from the perspective of my cockpit in just those light conditions. As soon as I saw this picture, I had to have it. I took the potentially dangerous step of buying a framed copy without asking my wife first! Fortunately, she loves it too and it has hung on the wall of our dining room ever since. I also own a copy of Robin's painting of the Lancaster, flanked by two D-Day veteran Spitfires, dropping one-million paper poppies over a ship carrying D-Day veterans to Normandy for the 60th anniversary of the Allied invasion. I was flying one of those Spitfires that day and so this portrays a memorable event in my life. I was also at the RAF Club in London, with Robin, when we presented the original of this painting to be hung in the Club.

I have often wished I had the wall space to hang more of Robin's aviation paintings, but now we can have them all in this wonderful book. Not only can we revel in the art, but in addition Robin provides us with explanatory notes with each picture, telling the historical background to the subject and giving some fascinating detail into his thoughts and his artist's 'tricks' in painting them. I am so pleased that he has decided to put this book, 'Painted Wings', together for our delight and I hope you enjoy it.

Clive Rowley

Introduction

I was born in 1949 in Lincolnshire. My parents were not rich by any means, and I distinctly remember my mum and dad looking like all those other post war people you see on the television box in black and white. Although their clothes were rarely new, they did try and look as smart as possible. My father had lots of low paid jobs but I had a happy childhood, partly I believe, because I was always doing something to keep myself occupied. In a 'Happy Childhood' sort of way I was always annoying mum and dad with things like making a noise with my model aircraft engines, or frightening the living daylights out of my mum with spooky gunpowder experiments. That one annoyed even me...I never quite got it right, always too much pesky burning and not enough lovely jubbly BANG!

I can't remember not being interested in aircraft. I must have been born with aircraft in my blood. Many aviation enthusiasts say they remember the day their father took them to an air show, and that was the beginning of their life-long interest. My earliest actual memory of aviation interest was of my favourite toy in the old cardboard box at primary school. This was an old battered Dinky Toy of a small nondescript plane. I can't remember what it was supposed to represent but who cared at that age...when it was in my hands, it flew! I remember even at this age, five years old, how annoyed I would be at friends charging around with models in their hands at ridiculous speeds, at the most implausible angles to the airflow, making noises like a crying baby. Mine was a real aeroplane in miniature. It flew gently to the ground; I even made a little squeak noise as it touched down.

Dad and myself, both model enthusiasts

I believe all this fascination for detail and realism originates from the fact that I was born in a village called Grimoldby, just a couple of hundred yards from the threshold of runway 24 at RAF Manby.

As RAF Manby was being constructed, my grandmother had a shop built on the main crossroads to serve the RAF personnel. My family and I lived above the shop until I was about five years old. Claim to fame…the crossroads has always been referred to as 'Smith's Corner' - it's in black and white as a bus route destination. Again very early memories - the sound of the four Avro Lincoln engines both fascinated me but also made me cry as I was trapped in my cot and not able to see what was making the noise. Night flying really annoyed me. As I got older, about four or five, the whole package fascinated me. The way the aircraft tilted backwards to touch down on all three wheels, the lovely little squeak as it touched down…I was five! It would be about this time in my life that I was actually thinking about the possibility of becoming a pilot. My interest in aviation was now set in stone.

My education was forged in a Secondary Modern school, 'High Holme Secondary Modern' in Louth, just five miles away from Grimoldby. I found education generally boring except for one or two subjects like technical drawing, art and woodwork. I loved the woodwork class because I loved working in wood. I loved art because you didn't have to do very much. Yes, it's true, I hated being told what to paint, but the teacher must have thought there was something in me that needed bringing out. All my boyhood time was taken up with model aircraft, with little time given to art. I was designing, building and flying radio controlled model aircraft still with the idea of becoming a pilot. Unfortunately, maths was never a strong subject in my early life, and although I did get a grade 1 in my GCSE,

My very first aeroplane painting

that didn't translate into a thorough enough knowledge to qualify as a pilot in the RAF. I did however qualify, upon applying, to become a Rolls Royce draughtsman apprentice at the jet engine place at Derby.

Becoming a draughtsman at R-R in 1966 was indeed quite an achievement in its own right for a Lincolnshire country boy. I tried to get into the Technical Illustration Department, but to no avail. Apparently, at the time, only university graduates were being accepted. This was a shame, as the job of draughtsman doing drawings of nuts and bolts more than half the time was incredibly boring. It has to be said, though, taking up an apprenticeship with Rolls Royce gave me the opportunity to join the R-R Merlin Flying Club at Hucknall just off the M1 north of Nottingham, and get my pilot's licence in 1968. This was the chance I had been waiting for all these years, and to be perfectly honest, nothing else in my life mattered at this stage. I took ownership of a beautiful little Auster and spent many wonderful hours towing gliders up at Church Broughton near Derby. I enjoyed just taking people up for a flight every now and again, one time a passenger being a police officer who wanted to investigate the presence of a suspicious aircraft flying over Darley Moor racetrack. The police thought it was someone smuggling drugs. He wanted me to fly alongside the suspicious aircraft whilst he held up his peaked cap to identify himself as the law. The drug trafficker turned out to be the owner of the racetrack! The police officer hadn't wasted his time taking his cap off, he was sick in it.

With a PPL under my belt I tolerated my apprenticeship to the end, but with storm clouds on the horizon in 1971 the big R-R crash came with the morale in the company at an all-time low. I decided to leave.

After experiencing the last few years, I felt I wanted a total change in my life. I actually chose to join the Royal Navy. Yes, this did shock some people at the time but, to be honest, I didn't want anything to do with the RAF unless it was as a pilot, and I have always had a subliminal, almost secret, interest in the sea. I continued to fly privately in the Navy, which quite fascinated folk as I was on the lower deck in terms of hierarchy. I found it really amusing on several occasions. Officers in particular either loved me for it or hated it. I took several of my shipmates flying from Compton Abass, just north of Portsmouth. That was real fun. My Skipper ended up wondering what on earth I was doing as a lower deck hand in the Navy. My intention was to serve my country long enough to save up enough money to buy my own house and leave the Navy with lots of great memories of a job well done. I did and I have.

Upon joining civilian life again, I found joining the Fire Service quite a natural move, as, at that time, a high proportion of new recruits were tradesmen or ex Royal Navy for some reason. I fitted in really well with the team at Nottingham Road Fire Station in Derby and thought this was to be my final career at last. With my background in draughtsmanship I was given several drawing and sign writing jobs within the station. It was, in fact, as a result of this that I attempted my first aviation painting, which I donated to the station. I knew at once, having completed the painting that this was what I was going to do with every spare moment. I was unaware at the time that an event was about to take place that would change the whole course of my life.

Called out to an emergency situation, involving a drunk driver trapped in his wrecked van in a ditch, I was on my way to the fire engine to remove a piece of cutting equipment, when unexpectedly the appliance (with its engine revving away driving a generator) clicked into gear and shot forward. I was knocked down, my helmet pulled off by the underside of the engine. The driver turned the wheel hard right, so my body was then between the front and double back wheels. The back wheels ran over my left foot and ankle. I was rushed to hospital in the same ambulance as the driver we were rescuing. The most dreadful thing about the whole episode was the indignity of being next to the driver in the hospital ward and, every time I was wheeled to an x-ray or treatment, he would yell "Dee Daa Dee Daa". Confounded bloke was in for two days. I was in for a month.

I had to retire as a result of my injury, but I was lucky enough to have a 'Cunning Plan'. As you may have guessed, it involved art. I had been thinking to myself for some time that in another world I would have been an artist. This was indeed my opportunity to custom build for myself, from scratch, a career that no one could take away from me. Even if, for some reason, I went totally blind, or had both hands cut off (blimey this is getting pessimistic!) I could go abstract with a brush in my mouth and probably get ten times more money for my work. Make that twenty.

In the beginning of my new career, I painted anything, because I just loved catching anything of interest on canvas, interpreting, in my own way, atmosphere and mood into a composition that would otherwise be quite plain. An example of embracing mood into an otherwise simple scenario, would be my painting 'Merlins in the Mist' I have done several paintings depicting sunsets and sunrises. Why not fog? It has attracted a lot of interest, as few paintings actually depict fog. Followers of my work have often asked me about painting fog and how I do it. This is something that is satisfyingly rewarding, as it takes a lot of practice. Catching certain tricky effects in a painting is a particularly frustrating thing as it usually means messing up a piece of work that up to that point, one is usually quite happy with, but, if you have the determination and patience, you will eventually crack it. This can be, in my opinion, the difference between a good artist and someone who struggles and gives up, not necessarily the basic art talent, but the background personality.

I joined the Guild of Aviation Artists in 1984 as a Friend, entering my first Guild exhibition with a painting of a Hawker Hart. It was rejected, so I obviously felt a little down at the time. My resultant thoughts turned into feelings of determination and that wonderful feeling of thinking "What do they know?", but of course they knew best, and I absorbed advice from a very reliable source. I followed up the next year with a 'Best Watercolour Trophy' which sealed my determination to do as well as I could in every annual show.

After just two years, I was voted a Full Member with letters after my name. I was very proud to receive this accolade and shortly after took over the responsibility of running the East Midlands Region of the Guild. Through this I met and made many friends. I enjoyed the regional meetings, basing the format on, if possible, acquiring the services of a personality in the world of art to give us a talk in the morning with a critique of Member's work in the afternoon.

I suppose really, to coin a phrase, the rest is history. My work has become more and more in demand as the years have gone by, with work in many prestigious locations, including the aviation museum of film director Peter Jackson. (He has actually commissioned me to do several paintings for him, and also purchased work from a major London Exhibition). Commissioned RAF work hangs in the Royal Air Force Club, Piccadilly, London, and work purchased from the Mall Galleries hangs in Hendon Royal Air Force Museum collection in London. Several of my pieces commissioned to celebrate anniversaries of RAF Squadrons adorn mess walls.

I still, however, love painting anything that demands atmosphere and mood - from misty mornings, to reflections in water whether it be a puddle on a patch of concrete, or the ever-changing moods of the sea. All this interest in landscape helps me tremendously with aviation work though, as I am drawn irresistibly to aircraft subjects on the ground. I find it rewarding to wrap a narrative around a subject, and this can be achieved, in my opinion, a little easier in a ground composition scattered with hardware, people, mess, equipment, mud and weeds etc. etc.

I hope my book will give pleasure to many people. I have enjoyed putting it together, and have tried to avoid the inevitable list of numbers/statistics/dates/facts etc etc, and embodied some of myself as a person and artist, passing over my thoughts and feelings that have resulted in a particular painting on the page you are reading.

I could not have planned a better life than I am living at the moment. I am lucky enough to have a job that is a passion. If I have learned one thing about life generally, it is this - if you are happy with what you are doing, and you are contented with your life, have no regrets. Everything you have done in the past, every wrong turn you have made, every bad decision you have come to, has helped to guide you to where you are today.

Early pilot days

The Paintings

'The End of the Chase'

DH2/Fokker Eindecker

The DH2 was a single seat pusher prop WWI fighter, the second design of the type following the DH1. Designed by Geoffrey de Havilland, the DH2 was the answer to what was known as the 'Fokker Scourge', the terrible impact the Fokker Eindecker had on British aircraft. The DH2 employed the use of a pusher propeller that allowed an uninterrupted forward firing Lewis gun. With multi side-mounted magazine pockets, it made a formidable opponent to the once superior enemy. Geoffrey de Havilland actually test flew his new creation himself.

The invention of the forward firing interrupter gear allowed a machine gun to fire through the propeller as it rotated, offering a much better chance of bringing a weapon to bear quickly on an enemy aircraft. The mechanism, more accurately known as gun synchronizer, was an idea that came to fruition in 1913/14, the creation of August Euler. He did, in fact, suggest the idea of a forward firing gun as early as 1910.

Aerial activity over the Western Front necessitated the use of a forward firing gun, so the Royal Flying Corps had to tolerate the pusher type of design, with the pilot of early DH2s having to transfer the gun from one mounting to another (there were three) whilst flying the aircraft. It surprisingly took a while for the 'powers that be' to come to the conclusion that it was easier to point the aircraft at the enemy and fire rather than pointing the swiveling gun and firing. Consequently, the DH2 eventually had a fixed forward firing .303 Lewis gun as shown.

The painting was commissioned by Chris Davey, an historic aviation novelist. The painting was the cover design for his novel 'Turner's Defence', chronicling the life and fortunes of young WWI pilot, Will Turner.

'In the collection of Mr Chris Davey'.

'Bombing Up Yorker'

Avro Lancaster

This painting depicts a Lancaster Mk. III powered by four Merlin engines. Assigned to 44 (Rhodesia) Squadron on 5th February 1944 at Dunholme Lodge Lincolnshire, KM-Y (Yorker) ND 578 was flown by Plt Off John Chatterton on its first fifteen operations, after which he received the DFC. In fact, the whole crew received the DFC after their tour. This was very unusual during the war, an award reflecting the heroism of the equally brave crew.

Y-Yorker completed its 100th sortie in February 1945 with Fg Off Hayler as skipper, surviving to complete its 123rd operation by 17/18th April with Harold Parkin in the driving seat, by this time stationed at Spilsby.

The significance of the "spade" nose art reflects the fact that John Chatterton was a farmer (a career that continued after the war) and it became his logo.

Unfortunately, his CO didn't approve of it, and it only lasted one week before it had to come off!

I have always been attracted to the cluster of glass concentrated at the front of the airframe of the Lancaster - the cockpit, front gun turret and the bomb aimer's dome. In certain light conditions, the glass attracts light from all directions and offers the artist a wonderful feature to focus on. I have painted several canvases depicting the front end of the Lancaster taking advantage of the way the Lancaster sits so beautifully on the ground.

One of the challenging elements of the painting was the rainbow. Due to a rainbow actually being reflected light from the sun, all aspects of the rainbow should be lighter than the background. Some artists don't appreciate this phenomenon, and just apply red/orange etc. paint on to the grey sky. This will more likely than not result in the red being darker in tone than the grey sky. The rainbow will appear even darker than the background, if the sky is quite bright. What is required is that the rainbow should firstly be painted white, and then a subtle application of the respective colours applied to that.

I was very proud to have my prints of this painting signed by both John Chatterton, and Harold Parkin, respectively the first and last skippers of 'Y-Yorker'. A rare coming together of two signatories made this a truly collectable print. I managed to organise the meeting of these two characters after so many years, concluding in a signing event featured on TV. This was a positive launch for my aviation art career.

The original was purchased at a large country show, the Stoneleigh Park 'Town and Country Festival' in Warwickshire. At time of purchase it was destined for Spain. 'Bombing Up Yorker' was actually the third aviation painting of my aviation art career, and it couldn't have given me a better start!

Oil on Canvas, sold privately, hanging in Spain at time of publication

‘Les Knight, The Final Attempt’

617 Squadron Lancaster

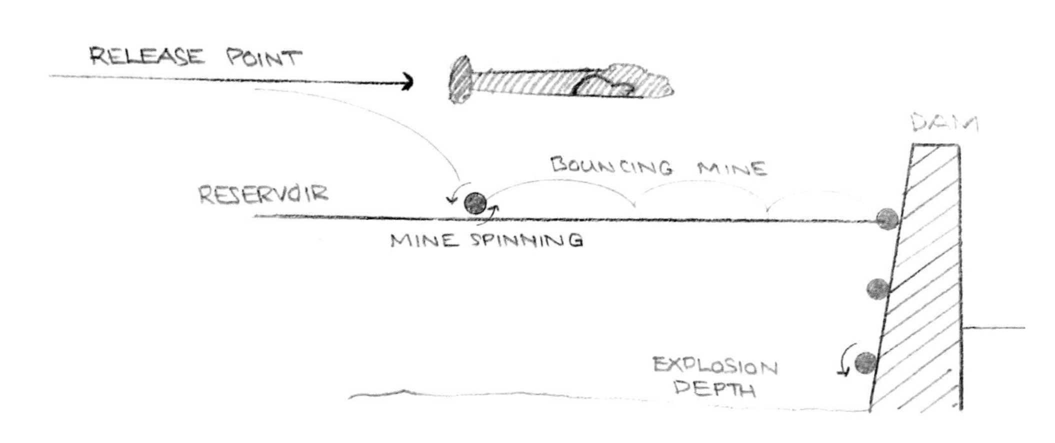

I was commissioned to produce this Dam Buster painting on the basis of the Eder Dam not having been painted quite so often as the Mohne Dam, the subject of the famous 1955 film, ‘The Dam Busters’. I just find it so difficult, even as a past pilot myself, to understand the task of not only flying at night in an area one has never been before, but having to do an extremely difficult job of work in your ‘office’, whilst being shot at by someone you have never met before whose intention it is to kill you. Les Knight’s run in was the last attempt at delivering a successful mine to destroy the dam, and my image depicts this low level attack.

The science and dynamics involved in the process of delivering a bouncing bomb that would destroy the dam was very complex, resulting in laboratory test facilities and test runs to determine the height, aircraft speed, and rate of backward rotation of the mine, to ensure the correct dam contact and subsequent ’sticking’ to the dam as it dropped to the optimum depth for explosion.

It was always going to be a difficult task destroying the dams, as the width of the wall thickened up considerably the deeper it went down. The scientists and engineers knew that the explosion shock waves that would be necessary to break up the fabric of the dam travel better through water, so the closer the mine was to the stone work upon exploding, the better. This was achieved by backward rotating the mine to ensure it stayed tightly in contact with the dam wall until it achieved the preset depth for detonation. The diagram illustrates this principle. The gyroscopic effect of a rapidly rotating cylinder also ensured the stable bounce characteristics of the mine, helping to guide it accurately to its target.

The actual position of observation for this composition was on a footpath that offers a good view of the dam, and also brings into play the opportunity to have a little foreground detail in the form of plant growth as shown. As I will always say, this is a good way of enhancing the effect of depth on a flat canvas and of course spreads the general interest further around the canvas.

Oil on Canvas, in the collection of Mr Paul Maton

‘Two Boys - One Dream’
Avro Lancaster

My painting ‘Two Boys - One Dream’ was a commission. The brief was for the composition to embody various elements, including two boys with bikes, and a bit of atmosphere with a Lancaster on the ground. This is the sort of commission I do like, when there is a lot for me to have a go at as an artist, from the start.

I personally think foregrounds in any ground view composition are of great importance, and this is a typical example. The fence posts, not in very good condition here and there, all add character and interest and lead the viewer to the two children with their bikes - this of course being quite a common practice during the war. With airfields often occupying what was, before the war, a farmer’s field, farmers’ wives were often seen taking breakfast or just a welcome cup of tea out to the most appreciative ground crews.

The Lancaster in the painting could, of course, be at one of many airfields during the war, as the extremities of the airfields looked very much the same. Often a commissioner will stipulate a particular airfield, pinned down by the visual presence of a church or farmhouse. This was to have been anywhere in Lincolnshire. The image shows an Avro Lancaster Mk III being prepared for yet another bombing mission over enemy lines. The turnround, involving bombing up, re-arming and the inevitable general maintenance, was very involved and labour intensive, but it all had to be done as quickly as possible as the aircraft and crew had to be flying again for the next night sortie.

The workload for all concerned was relentless, and many people forget just how hard the ground crew, or ‘Erks’ as they were known, suffered in the cold conditions.

Oil on Canvas, in the collection of Dr Peter Stell

‘Hungry and Thirsty’

Avro Lancaster

Depicting an Avro Lancaster Mk III, my painting was inspired by the fact that I do actually love painting snow, and, yes, I do love painting the Lancaster. I owe a lot to the designer Roy Chadwick for designing what transpires to be, in my opinion, one of the most beautiful aeroplanes ever designed. Everything about it attracts me. The well-proportioned fuselage terminates at the rear with a pair of nicely shaped and proportioned fin/rudder combinations. Even the length of the undercarriage oleo legs and diameter of the tyres allows the aircraft to sit so beautifully on the ground, and offers an attractive view of the aircraft from any angle. I am still discovering new angles and directions to view familiar aircraft from. This is one of the advantages of building scale models. It is important to know, however, the shortcomings of working with models. Take note of the wing dihedral angles and the cockpit shapes. Note that tyres flatten considerably at the point of contact with the ground and just have a quick look from the front to see if all the flying surfaces are square and level. If plastic models are used for preliminary references, they are incredibly useful, as the outline profiles are usually very accurate and help with the initial basic build up at the early composition stage.

One thing I like about painting snow, is the fact that the only way one can depict the formation of the snow with its lumps and gullies, peaks and troughs, is the simple addition of shadows. Take away all the blue shading and you are just left with a sheet of white canvas. What a boring painting that would be.

Oil on Canvas, in the collection of Mr Daniel Sheehan

‘Too Low-Too Slow’

Avro Lancaster 617 Squadron

The Avro Lancaster was the most versatile heavy bomber of the war. Within its design remit, the aircraft was capable of delivering a load of large High Capacity ‘Cookies’ of up to 12,000lb each, or a bomb bay full of H.C. 500lb conventional bombs, the load commonly taken over Germany for the purpose of industrial destruction. Indeed, with an uninterrupted bomb bay of 33ft, the Lancaster often carried a combination of ordnance suited to the requirements of the sortie. Mines were carried, varying from magnetic to acoustic types, for attacks on submarines. Probably one of the most historically memorable loads carried by the Lancaster, was the dam destroying mine, the ‘Bouncing Bomb’ or ‘Upkeep’. Conceived by Barnes Wallis, the concept was rejected upon first introduction to the relevant authorities. Fighting his corner, he eventually managed to persuade the hierarchy to allow him to pursue his idea - a bomb that, when dropped from a travelling aircraft, would bounce like a stone skimmed across the water, strike the dam, explode at a certain depth and hopefully destroy the dam. Small-scale experiments were carried out in a laboratory, culminating in full-scale tests dropping full sized mines from Lancasters. The final tests (in fact just four days before the actual attack) were carried out at Reculver, off the coast of Kent.

In daylight at Reculver, the Lancasters would fly at a certain altitude at a certain speed, with the mines revolving backwards at a certain rate, and basically just see what happened. My painting depicts one of the chosen Lancasters (an appropriate number of Lancasters were modified to carry the mines, plus a rotating mechanism) dropping one of the mines. Early attempts revealed the aircraft were not flying at the correct speed and height. The splash was striking the tail area of the Lancaster and actually on one occasion damaged the tailplane and elevator, the Rear Gunner Sgt Norman Burrows must have got quite a shock! As Les Munro (one of the Dam Raid pilots) commented, “We are flying too low and too slow”. The height was increased to 60ft with the speed increased to 240mph. This was the perfect combination and was subsequently adopted. Les Munro liked my painting so much, he volunteered to personally sign a batch of prints for me. These prints quickly sold out, but I did have the great pleasure of having a further batch of limited edition prints signed by Eric Quinney, pilot of P-Popsie in the 1955 film ‘The Dam Busters’. ‘Popsie’ was Mick Martin’s aircraft and Eric can be seen flying the Lancaster on the left of the three Lancs, seen together flying low over the sea in the film.

I also have the honour of film director Sir Peter Jackson purchasing the original painting. It now hangs in his personal collection. He is truly an historic aviation fan.

Eric was with me at a show signing prints, and he and David Shepherd (a very pleasant surprise visit) are seen talking to each other at my sales unit at Sandringham, with my wife Carol in the background.

Oil on Canvas, in the collection of Sir Peter Jackson

‘Sunset Saviours’

Avro Lancaster MkIIIs

The mainstay of our bomber force during WWII was, of course, the Avro Lancaster, partly due to the inimitable reliability of the four Rolls Royce Merlin engines, and simply having a very large bomb bay, 33ft long.

It was originally a two-engined airframe, looking quite like the Lancaster, only missing two engines. The original two-engined ‘Lancaster’ was called the Manchester. It suffered terribly from a lack of power and reliability. Its engines were Rolls Royce Vulture 24-cylinder X-block units composed of two 12-cylinder V-block Royce Peregrines, one on top of the other. Lack of development and reliability assigned the Manchester to the scrap heap. The basic design as a bomb carrying platform was so attractive, though, that it was always going to be ripe for development and improvement into a successful aircraft. The result became the Lancaster.

Lancasters started out their RAF careers basically committed to daylight missions. The advantages of daylight operations are obvious, but suffered from the disadvantage of the bomber force being vulnerable to enemy attack. Losses were great, but with the advent of America joining the war, the B17 Flying Fortress was deemed more appropriate for the duty of daylight raids, leaving the Lancaster to carry out bombing raids at night.

The depicted Lancaster EM-M of 207 Sqn was the mount of Flt Lt Wallace McIntosh, DFC and Bar, DFM. McIntosh held throughout the war the record for kills from his rear turret, a total of eight. He wrote a book about his exploits titled ‘Gunning for the Enemy’. I had the pleasure and honour of visiting Wallace at his home in Aberdeen, during which time he personally signed all of my 500 limited prints. Unfortunately, he passed away in 2007. He is sadly missed.

Oil on Canvas, in the collection of Dr Peter Stell

‘Derwent Dam, Practice Run’

Avro Lancaster 617 Squadron

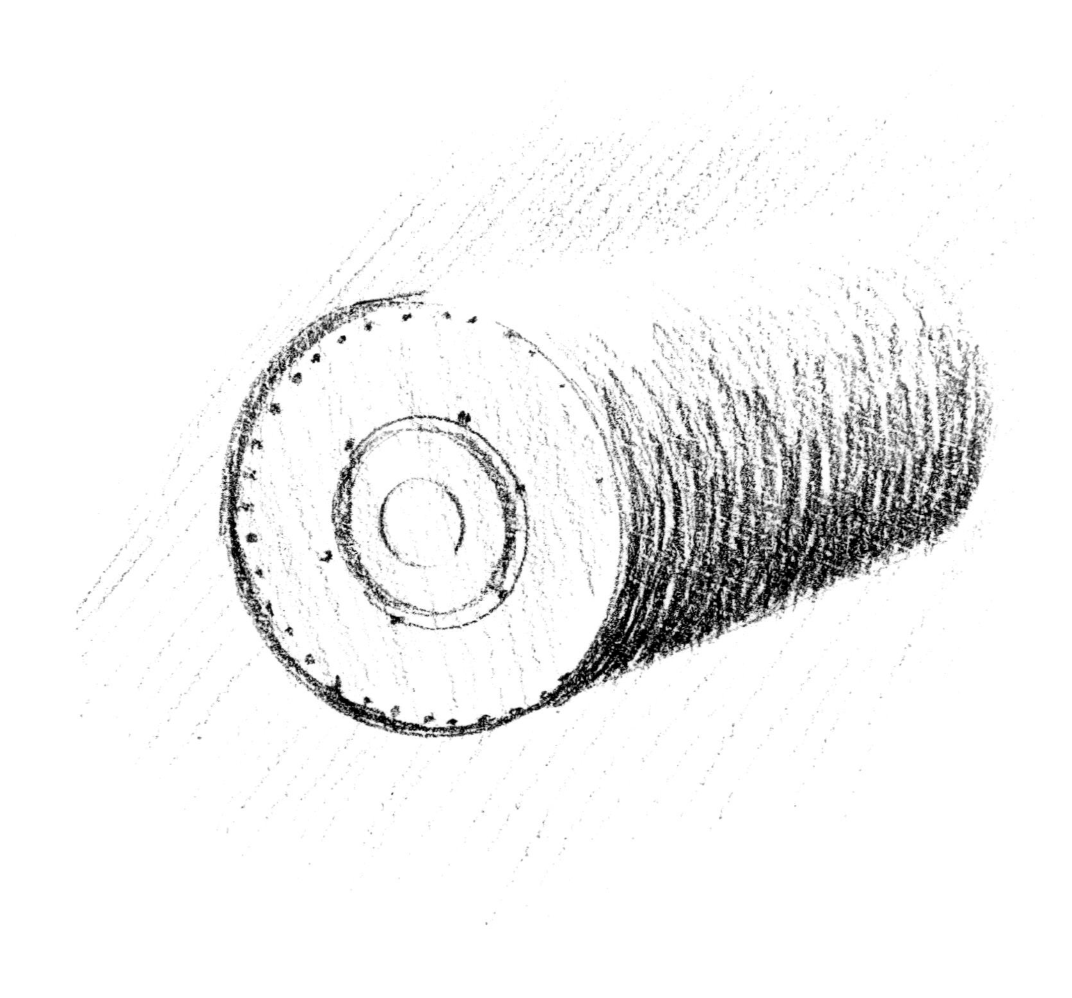

The Derwent Dam in the north of Derbyshire was a location for the practice runs for the German dam attacks. The towers offered a good simulation for the practice approaches and a valuable exercise for the bomb aimer. Logbook entries referred to the activities as “low flying practice”, as it had to be kept very secret. In order to confuse the Fifth Columnist activity present in the UK at the time, 617 Squadron practiced low flying runs in the Lake District at several locations. There was a period of time spent at Reculver in Kent just four days before the attacks, determining the optimum speed and height of the aircraft for good mine bounce performance.

Flt Lt Shannon piloted the Lancaster AJ-L. The first aircraft to attempt an attack on the Eder dam, AJ-L made several unsuccessful attempts at lining up to drop the bomb, hampered by the difficult approach to the dam. After allowing AJ-Z to drop its bomb, AJ-L made a final successful attack on the dam, its bomb exploding accurately, but failing to cause a breach. The aircraft returned to base safely.

I paid a visit to the dam for accurate references prior to starting the painting. I have just enhanced the foreground grass a little to add interest at the bottom of the image. I do think foregrounds are of paramount importance in paintings as they can, in most instances, give the eye something to look at before one’s attention is drawn into the painting, adding an illusion of distance and depth.

It is interesting to note that the piece of wood with two nails used as an alignment instrument for assessing the release point (seen in the film) was never used. Trials determined that vibration in the nose of the aircraft was too severe rendering the instrument useless. A loose piece of string attached across the bomb aimer’s space pulled tight with relevant markings on the blister was far more effective.

Oil on Canvas

‘Cold Hands Everywhere’
Avro Lancaster

The Lancaster bomber during the war had to be looked after and maintained with the same attention, regardless of the weather conditions. Crews worked in terrible conditions during the winter, with hands so cold, but tasks had to be completed. My time in the Royal Navy, many times on the upper deck in freezing weather, allows me to appreciate what they had to tolerate. The small hut to the right in the painting is their only refuge from the wind and cold. That Lancaster has got to be ready!

The Lancaster shown is KM-Q, LM592 of 44 (Rhodesia) Squadron, unfortunately shot down outbound over Holland, crashing with all crew killed, near the village of Riethoven in Noord-Brabant The unfortunate mission started with a take-off time of 22:57 from 44 Squadron’s airfield at Dunhome Lodge. The aircrew were-

Pilot: Plt Off Edwin Albert Canty RAAF age 29
Flight Engineer: Sgt Ronald Edgar Clay age 19
Navigator: Fg Off John Reuben Vowles RAAF
Bomb Aimer: Sgt Eric Norris RAFVR age 22
Wireless Operator: Fg Off Walter Marshall Crook RAFVR age 22
Mid-Upper Gunner: Sgt Ernest George Scott RAFVR age 20
Rear Gunner: Flt Sgt Louis Joseph Patrick McCoy RAAF age 20

Having studied the beautiful forms and shapes of the Lancaster, the history of its conception and manufacture, and as an artist embodying all these elements of landscape sky and composition to hopefully result in a rewarding painting, I find myself at the end writing a list of seven young men who died on that night for us all. Looking at their ages, one can only be left in awe at the thought of having to climb into the fuselage of that aircraft night after night, flying in the dark over an enemy country full of people who want to kill you.

Oil on Canvas, in the collection of Captain Darryl Elliott

‘Towards the End’

Avro Lancaster B1 Special

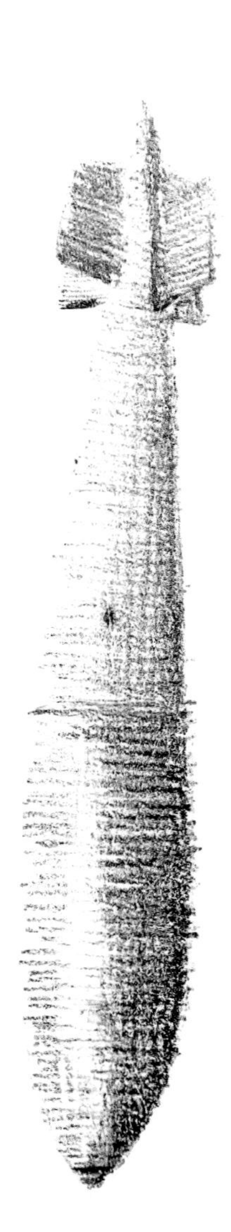

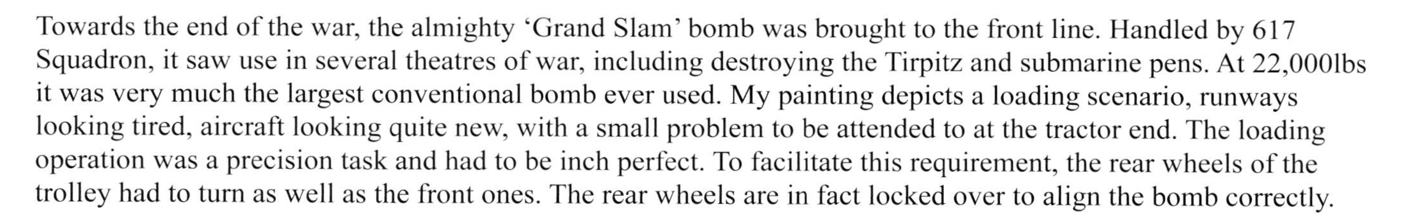

Towards the end of the war, the almighty ‘Grand Slam’ bomb was brought to the front line. Handled by 617 Squadron, it saw use in several theatres of war, including destroying the Tirpitz and submarine pens. At 22,000lbs it was very much the largest conventional bomb ever used. My painting depicts a loading scenario, runways looking tired, aircraft looking quite new, with a small problem to be attended to at the tractor end. The loading operation was a precision task and had to be inch perfect. To facilitate this requirement, the rear wheels of the trolley had to turn as well as the front ones. The rear wheels are in fact locked over to align the bomb correctly.

There was a plethora of engineering problems to solve as a result of the Lancaster carrying such a large bomb. How would the massive ten-ton bomb be held in position, and how would it be released? Interestingly, the bomb was simply held in position by a single huge, thick, chain slung from side to side in the bomb bay. A heavy-duty precision-engineered release link then broke away, allowing the chain to be flung to one side with the bomb dropping free. If one looks closely at the moment of release in one of several archive photographs, the chain can be seen hanging down.

There was a complex bomb loading procedure, as can be imagined. I had to take a special trip to the RAF Museum at Hendon, London, to get up close and personal to one of the preserved bomb trolleys used for the job. It was amazingly complex. It was an engineering masterpiece in its own right!

The subject Lancaster in the painting is a Lancaster B Mk1 Special, with modifications that were necessary for the transportation and delivery of such a large bomb. The mid upper and front gun positions were removed to save weight. I never thought that this was the best-looking Lancaster, but it did represent a fighting machine with a serious job to do, and brought to the fore the thought that the war was coming to an end.

Bomb general spec.-
Weight: 22,000lb (10,000kg)
Length: 26ft 6in (8.08m)
Diameter: 3ft 10in (1.16m)
Filling: Torpex
Filling weight: 9,136lb (4,144kg)
Penetration: 130ft (40m) earth, 20ft (6.1m) concrete
Blast yield: 6.5 tons TNT equivalent

Oil on Canvas, hanging in a private collection in Australia

‘Snowbound Lancasters’

Avro Lancaster MkIII

One of the many Lincolnshire Lancaster Association’s commissions, published as a fine art print and Christmas card. Requested every year, it was quite a challenge thinking of something different every time.

Fortunately, from a visual image point of view, the nose of the Lancaster is incredibly attractive with the cluster of glass concentrated in the nose area. This dictated the basic composition of the painting, bringing into view the two port engines with all the detail they have to offer. The Lancaster sits very prettily on its two main wheels with its nose sniffing the air like a wild animal raring to go. With the airframe sitting back on its tail wheel, the far Lancaster has a good position on the canvas balancing the composition and adding important interest without interfering too much with the foreground Lancaster.

I have never been afraid of a dark grey sky in my paintings, if that is what suits it best. In my painting ‘Snowbound Lancasters’ I have introduced, in the background sky, a hint of a snow shower dropping down from the cloud base. All very intimidating and moody!

Again, as mentioned briefly in one or two other commentaries in this book, foreground was considered very important in this painting too. As can be seen, if there was little or no foreground detail, there would be an awkward open space with little to draw one’s attention, especially in the bottom left corner. Trees were added encroaching into view from the left, to lift detail at this location above the horizon line, again balancing the composition. It has been quite amusing on several occasions in the past, talking to people who have bought the print, pointing out to them that there is a small snowman in front of the aircraft with the wheel chock rope going over his arm. I was actually going to call the painting ‘Chocks Away’ but we stuck with the LLA title ‘Snowbound Lancasters’.

Oil on Canvas, commissioned by the Lincolnshire Lancaster Association

‘Disturbing the Peace’
Avro Lancaster MkIII

As the heavy horses are fed, the peace and tranquillity of the event is rudely interrupted by the intrusion of a Lancaster coming in to land after an all-important test flight. The scenario does, of course, illustrate quite clearly (although the farmer at this moment may be feeling a little cross) the way in which all walks of life pulled together to achieve the ultimate goal... success over the enemy in achieving victory.

The canvas was commissioned by the Lincolnshire Lancaster Association for their 2011 Fine Art Print and Christmas card. Happily, the original sold very quickly at the Guild of Aviation Artists Exhibition at the Mall Galleries in London.

The painting features a Lancaster Mk III coming in to land quite awkwardly over a peaceful scene somewhere in Lincolnshire. I try, if possible, to wrap some sort of narrative around a scene, which can attract the attention of people who may not necessarily be interested in aviation. As with this scenario, there has been a lot of interest from people who have an association with horses.

The location is typical of the Lincolnshire landscape and typical of the views associated with WWII airfield localities, so my landscape prowess came to the fore, involving one of my favourite landscape elements, snow.

I find snow a fascinating substance to paint with all the lumps and bumps, gullies and grooves, sculptured in it. When all is said and done, the shapes and texture in the snow are visually created only because of the shadows and shading that fall upon it. As can be seen, the shadow and shading rendition in the ditch is quite dominating, and adds density and weight to the lower portion of the image. This compensates for the Lancaster presence in the upper portion of the image.

Oil on Canvas, sold at the Guild of Aviation Artists Annual Exhibition, Mall Galleries, London

‘Avro Shackleton MR3’

A true workhorse of the RAF was indeed the Avro Shackleton. One of the many duties of the Shackleton was long-range maritime patrol. The design concept can be traced back in a very family tree sort of way. In one respect it started out life as the well-known Avro Lancaster. This then developed into the Avro Lincoln which, after a short period of time, became the Avro Shackleton.

A commission for an ex Shackleton pilot, my painting depicts a typical air sea rescue mission. Having dropped a smoke flare, the aircraft flies downwind / crosswind of the stricken vessel. Lindholme gear is then released which consists of a nine-man inflatable dinghy connected by two floating ropes several hundred feet long with survival packs on the ends. The survivors then wind drift into the ropes and haul in the gear.

The composition of the picture was assisted by the top of the fuselage simply being white, contrasting with the dark sea. It is always good to be able to contrast light with dark in any composition as it adds depth and interest. It is quite surprising how effectively just a small amount of light can enhance a painting that would otherwise be composed of totally dark elements. A particularly good example of this is the still life painting of the helmet and goggles featured in this book. I had the pleasure of meeting Sqn Ldr Dick Woodhead, ex Shackleton pilot of 120 Squadron, Kinloss, who gave me a great amount of help explaining the complexities of the Lindholme gear, and the hardship experienced during long noisy flights, sometimes of 20 hours’ duration.

The painting shows a Shackleton of 120 Squadron, Kinloss.

Basic career summary for the Shackleton-

Service 1951-1991
Operators-Royal Air Force/South African Air Force.
Manufactured 1951-1958
Quantity built 185

Oil on Canvas, commissioned by 120 Squadron Shackleton Pilot

'Team Olympus'

Avro Vulcan

Martin Withers, Vulcan Captain, poses for me

My initial thought behind the painting 'Team Olympus' was to capture the characteristics that so many people adore and, in many cases, remember the Vulcan for - the beautiful wing shape, many times the area of a lot of people's gardens, and the signature 'howl' of those four Rolls Royce Olympus engines at full throttle. Quite a sound that many people heard in the Cold War years. It is not understood by many people that, for all this noise, the Vulcan's engines never did have afterburners (reheat).

The Vulcan's first flight was in 1952, and it operated until 1984. This statistic in itself is of great interest as it brings to light the fact that there was only a gap of seven years between the Avro Lancaster and the Avro Vulcan. A truly remarkable achievement when one compares the technological advancements involved in the conception, design and construction of the Vulcan compared to the Lancaster.

It was, of course, designed and operated as a deterrent to the Russian nuclear threat, and was never intended to be a first strike aircraft. Looking at the situation from a slightly different angle, if it had been necessary to send the Vulcans over to Russia to deliver the nuclear weapon they were designed to carry, the whole investment would have been a total waste of time and money. In other words, the Vulcans performed a perfect job - they were never used in a nuclear theatre of war.

The Vulcan started out life as a B1 and was first delivered to the RAF in 1956. The improved B2 was delivered in 1960, sporting improved engines of higher performance, a larger wing area, and, of course, the inevitable improved electronics. At that time the Vulcan formed one third of the British V Bombers nuclear deterrent Force, the other two being the Handley Page Victor, and the Vickers Valiant.

My painting depicts XH558, at the time the only flying example of the type in the world. XH558 participated in its last season of shows in 2015 after years of re-build to flying condition. Having been operated during its air show career from Doncaster Sheffield (Robin Hood) Airport (ex RAF Finningley), it now resides there permanently as a taxi-able example, awaiting her new role as part of the VTTS exciting new Aviation Academy project.

Oil on Canvas, in the collection of Mr Jeff Carpenter

‘At the Going Down of the Sun’

Battle of Britain Memorial Flight

Commissioned by the Battle of Britain Memorial Flight, the painting was to include the three main types of aircraft that were instrumental in the struggle during WWII, these aircraft being the Supermarine Spitfire (the furthest single engine aircraft), the Hawker Hurricane (closest aircraft) and the Avro Lancaster bomber. The Spitfire and Hurricane were the main aircraft participating in the Battle of Britain, but given the enormity and indeed, the rarity of the Lancaster, being only one of two surviving in the world still flying, it was always going to be part of the collection, and is, in fact, considered to be the ‘Head Boy’.

The collection started in a very loose manner with various aircraft types scattered about in a variety of hangars, but, as many members of the public will see now, it is a well organised concern, based at RAF Coningsby. A large dedicated hanger houses all the aircraft and serves as the maintenance workshop, with well-trained RAF personnel constantly seen repairing and maintaining the well-loved and cherished historic icons.

It all really started in 1957, when the last three remaining flying Spitfires that were at the disposal of the RAF were flown to Biggin Hill. On 11th July 1957 the three aircraft were embraced in the organisation known then as the Historic Aircraft Flight, now known as the Battle of Britain Memorial Flight or BBMF.

Very few colours were used in the painting of this canvas as the overriding colour and light was generated by a setting sun, this of course resulting in a red cast to a greater or lesser degree all over the image. I always find this can be an advantage when showing a collection of work, as inevitably several of the paintings will be composed of many colours, adding interest to the collection, revealing the artist to have quite a flexible palette.

Photos on this page show the preliminary pencil sketch, and myself invited into the BBMF hangar to study the airframes in detail. These were still shots lifted from a video filming me painting the canvas. A film company, ITVV, visited me in my studio to capture the whole process from start to finish. The film was supposed to give the impression of the painting taking something like a couple of weeks to do. Unfortunately, the film crew could only visit at irregular intervals and the process took a couple of months or so giving the impression that my hair grows much quicker than anyone else’s!

Oil on Canvas, in the Collection of Captain Nick Stein

‘60th Anniversary D-Day Poppy Drop’

Battle of Britain Memorial Flight

I was commissioned by the Lincolnshire Lancaster Association, in conjunction with the Battle of Britain Memorial flight, to paint this canvas. The image depicts Lancaster PA474 along with Spitfire MK356 and AB910 dropping one million poppies over MV Van Gogh off the coast of Normandy, commemorating the invasion of the Normandy beaches in June 1944.

AB910 continued to fly operationally up to July 1944, serving with 242, 416 and 402 (RCAF) Squadrons, flying numerous cover patrols with the latter over the D-Day invasion beaches on 6th June 1944 and afterwards.

Spitfire MK356 joined the war on 14th April 1944 piloted by twenty-year-old, Fg Off Gord Ockenden in action over occupied France. MK356 was subsequently involved in sweeps and ground attacks, both bombing and low level strafing, in preparation for the D-Day invasion. MK356 continued its offensive presence in support of ground troops after the invasion.

The event was witnessed by veterans of D-Day on board the Van Gogh as the Lancaster released the petals from the gaping bomb bay. Notice how the wind direction would drift the petals over the ship.

One of the main problems to solve when painting the picture was interpreting the limited photos of the Van Gogh taken from the rear turret of the Lancaster. The angle of the ship had to be changed to allow it to sit convincingly on the sea and combine with the angle of the Lancaster. I decided on a steep angle looking down on the Lancaster as this gave me the opportunity to slightly overlap the ship with it’s wing tip, helping to tie the composition together.

It was commented that the poppies in the painting followed exactly the pattern on the day, lifting slightly a hundred yards or so after they came out of the bomb bay before they began to fall.

Oil on Canvas, hanging in the RAF Club, London

‘Mission Accomplished’

Boeing B17 Flying Fortress

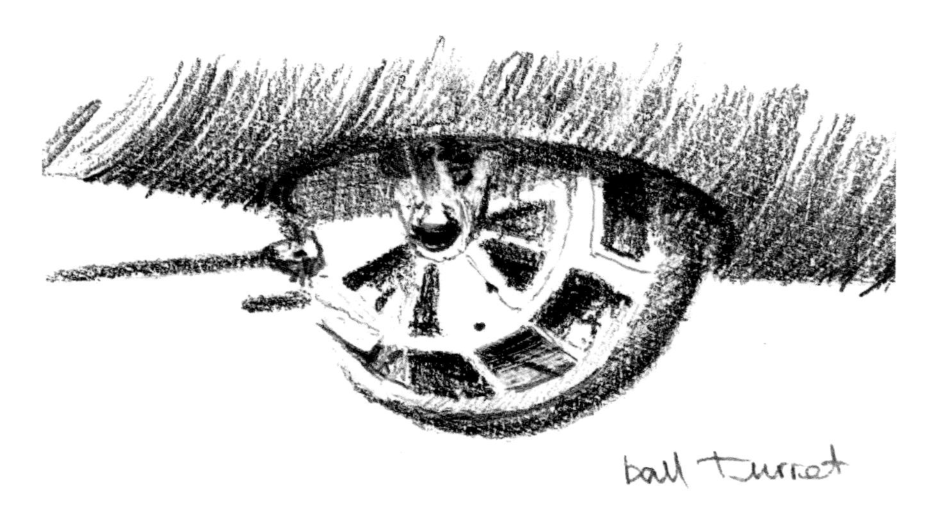

The Flying Fortress was a heavy strategic bomber built by Boeing in the United States. Its first flight was on the 28th July 1935 and it came into active service in April 1938. Its primary function during the war was precision daylight heavy bombing, targeting German industry and munitions. Based at many RAF airfields in Britain, the B17 with its daylight missions, complemented the Avro Lancaster of the RAF with its night-time offensive strategy. The Fortress did participate to a certain degree in the Pacific theatre, conducting attacks on the Japanese.

Although the main duty of the Fortress was to drop as many bombs as possible on the enemy, it was taken advantage of, with its size and versatility, for several other military duties, such as dropping propaganda leaflets, food supplies, and life rafts to ditched aircrew.

The B17 surprisingly survived in service until 1968 flying with the Brazilian Air Force. It was produced between 1936 and 1945. In all, a total of 12,731 were built.

The painting shows two of the classic Flying Fortresses during a descent from 18,000ft. The B17Gs are of the 379th Bomb Group, 525th Bomb Squadron. These two aircraft, unfortunately, after a successful raid over enemy territory, collided with each other shortly before arrival at their destination.

The sky in this painting is one of the most satisfying, being cumulus clouds, the product of columns of rising warm air that produce those lovely cauliflower cloud heads. I remember well, as a young pilot, flying around the tops of these clouds having great fun.

Whilst doing the research for the painting, I did dwell on various design aspects of the airframe, and looked carefully at the ball turret underneath the fuselage. I actually looked at it more closely than ever before and came to the conclusion that it was a brilliant piece of kit. I never realised just how small it was, and the incredible effort it must have taken just getting into the thing, let alone having to do a job of work once you were settled.

Oil on Canvas, in the collection of Mr Geoff Burke

‘Rapid Response’
Boeing Chinook

The Boeing Chinook is truly a military workhorse with a lifting capability consistent with the arduous requirements of the Army in action. I have chosen to depict the Chinook in a desert scenario, revealing just enough of the airframe to instantly distinguish the type. This would, of course, be a truly credible composition for a painting, as the Chinook would kick up an awful lot of sand and dust. This is just up my street as an artist. I feel it captures the essence of movement, sound and drama, making it a very exciting canvas to paint. From the start, the essence of the image was going to be the dust cloud. It is indeed, not a painting of a Chinook, but a painting of a Chinook at work.

I am always truly amazed when I see the incredible performance of the Chinook at air shows. How can such a lumbering, chunky, lump of metal do all those things? I sometimes just can’t watch, out of fear. I have a reasonable understanding of physics and dynamics, but still can’t understand how those massive rotor discs spinning at such a high rate, tolerate such a rapid change of direction. I don’t think the Chinook was ever told of gyroscopic forces!

At time of print, the RAF is the largest operator of the type outside the United States of America, with much action history associated with Afghanistan, Iraq, peacekeeping activity in the Balkans, and, of course, the well documented action in the Falkland Islands. Three of the Chinooks that were present at the Falklands on the vessel MV Atlantic Conveyor went down with the ship after the infamous enemy attack on 25th May 1982, when the ship was struck by two Exocet missiles in the port quarter.

Probably the best known Chinook is BN (Bravo November) of 18 Squadron. This particular Chinook earned its reputation having served in every theatre of action the RAF has participated in during the 25 years of service to date. Actions include the Falkland Islands, Germany, Northern Ireland, Lebanon, Afghanistan and Iraq. On one famous occasion during the Falklands conflict, BN lifted eighty-one fully loaded paratroopers, twice its normal capacity, then it returned to Goose Green to pick up another seventy-five!

Oil on Canvas, sold at the Guild of Aviation Artist Exhibition, Mall Galleries, London

‘The Successful Business Trip’

Bristol Beaufighter

It may seem to many people that Coastal Command was an easy, safe job. After all, it was given coastal duties. To many people, this mistakenly meant sticking to the coast. Not the case as aircraft types such as the Catalina and Sunderland went far out to sea. North Coates Strike Wing, based on the North Lincolnshire coast, suffered more fatalities than any other Wing.

My painting depicts a heavily armed trawler being attacked by a Bristol Beaufighter from the North Coates Strike Wing. The effort of the Strike Wing during the war was to severely cripple the German war effort by cutting off the supply of raw materials to the manufacturing industry.

Many thousands of tons of shipping were destroyed by these attacks, but sadly at great cost. Anti-shipping operations, such as the one shown, suffered the highest percentage losses within Coastal Command, with heavily armed merchant ships, including innocent looking trawlers, filling the sky with anti-aircraft flak.

I was inspired to paint my picture after being commissioned to produce a painting for a reunion of Strike Wing Association members - a formal formation of all three squadrons (254, 143, and 236) that operated at the same time during the war. I was amazed at the bravery of those men and felt, having spoken to several members of the Strike Wing Association, that an action scene had to be caught in paint. Having seen several paintings of the Beaufighter in a similar situation, I rose to the challenge of catching the Beaufighter from a rearward aspect.

I hope my efforts will help to perpetuate and nurture the memory of the airmen, navigators and pilots who gave their lives for us and, of course, those who were lucky enough to have survived.

The canvas obviously includes sea and lots of it. In the summary text of several other subjects in this book I do make mention of the fact that I love painting the sea. To be honest, I do actually like painting any water, whether it is a puddle in a road or waves smashing over a lighthouse. I love the energy and dynamics of moving water, as it adds interest into any subject, whether it be aviation, marine or landscape.

Oil on Canvas

‘Desert Training, Abu Sueir 1944’

Curtiss Kittyhawk

Fg Off Drew

The aircraft shown opposite in my painting was flown by Fg Off Drew who, conveniently living near to where I live, signed a few of my limited edition prints. Although the painting depicts an aviation training scenario, there were indeed several serious accidents, including two of Fg Off Drew’s fellow pilots who were killed.

The aircraft was an American built unit of all metal construction. The basic specification was of single seat monoplane configuration, housing a large single engine, the Allison V-1710. With an unexpected low performance at higher altitudes due to its single-stage, single-speed supercharger, it was mainly used in a ground attack role.

The Kittyhawk made its first flight in 1938, retiring in 1948. Its top speed was 360 mph, with a range of 650 miles.

It is always a challenge introducing interest and content into a painting such as this, where there is inevitably an awful lot of sand and the expected blue sky. Thankfully with the blast of the propeller there is a cloud of sand blown up to add movement and added texture to the composition. I always feel it adds interest to a painting when there is the possibility of having detail obscured by dust or smoke as in this case, or even more so in the painting ‘The Rail Strike’ where there was a lot of work and effort just covered up by the smoke. All adds to the overall completed effect.

Oil on Canvas, in the collection of Mr Jeremy Drew

'The Thorn in the Side'

de Havilland Mosquito

This project was a commission by David Bownes, who is one of the chaps who worked on restoring this beautiful aircraft to its present state (now on show at the RAF Museum Cosford). It sports the distinctive bulge under the fuselage that allowed the aircraft to carry the 4,000lb 'Cookie' blast bomb.

Personnel in the British Air Ministry strongly objected to the building of it, but from the day production finally began in 1941, the Royal Air Force never had enough Mosquitoes to perform the incredible variety of tasks that air tacticians envisaged for this amazing aeroplane. It excelled at day and night bombing from high or very low altitudes, long-range reconnaissance, air-to-air combat in daylight and darkness, and finding and striking distant targets at sea. No less than forty two distinct versions of the DH 98 entered service. At speeds higher than most fighters, Mosquitoes carried heavy loads great distances because of two key design features: a lightweight, streamlined, wooden airframe propelled by powerful, reliable engines. The Mosquito, nicknamed 'The Wooden Wonder', was constructed from timber, including, amazingly, Ecuadorian balsa, glued and screwed together in innovative ways. The design package was completed with the inclusion of the world's finest power plants, a pair of Rolls Royce Merlins. This aeroplane was a fine example of an innovative concept built during the war.

Seeing the actual aircraft on display at Cosford aviation museum was fascinating and sort of weird. I just had to cheekily step over the barrier rope and run my hand across the airframe. Like it really came as a surprise…it was wood! I just could not imagine the forces the wooden structure would have been experiencing during a fast flight. I was looking at nothing more than a 100% scale radio controlled model.

Oil on Canvas, in the collection of Mr David Bownes

‘The Rail Strike’

de Havilland Mosquito

‘The Rail Strike’ depicts a de Havilland Mosquito V attacking the rail yard installation at Nantes, France in June 1944. Eleven Mosquitoes went into action, chosen aircraft going in at an altitude of 60ft. As you can imagine, one of the main dangers encountered during such action was, in fact, flying through the smoke caused by previous attacks.

The superior performance of the Mosquito was due to several elements, but primarily the streamlined front form of the airframe, light construction (one only has to see the way quite large sections of airframe are easily carried around the factory floor during construction) and, of course, the ever-reliable Rolls Royce Merlin engines.

Letters ‘GB’ represents 105 Squadron, first formed at Andover, Hampshire, on 23rd September 1917 as part of the Royal Flying Corps. Disbanded in 1920, 105 Squadron reformed at Harwell in 1937 and in 1942 was the first Squadron to receive the new Mosquito.

The temptation to leave most of the rail yard exposed had to be resisted and the majority of the canvas was covered in smoke. This was quite a challenge, as smoke moves and dissipates in a very natural way, demanding concentration from one end of the canvas to the other. One has only to study the archive photos from the war to see the effect of the smoke; I felt this had to be interpreted on canvas.

Throughout my career, at some point I have always been asked, “Do you paint the aircraft first, and then the background?” It varies from artist to artist, but for me the only way is to paint the background first and then the subject.

The highlights and shading on the aircraft depend on the quality of the environment the subject is sitting in. I would find it quite annoying having to paint the landscape background with its sun direction, and general mood dependent on the appearance of the aircraft. I have always considered the background just as important as the main subject. An example of this is the painting ‘Cold War 1941’, and in rare, but memorable, cases, I have enjoyed the background more than painting the aircraft. I am after all an artist, not just a painter of aircraft.

Oil on Canvas

'Thunder at Dawn'

de Havilland Mosquitoes 105 Squadron

In December 1941 105 Squadron took up residence at RAF Horsham St. Faith, near Norwich, Norfolk (nowadays better known as Norwich International Airport) The Squadron took a short break from battle in order to train its crews on the new Mosquito Mk IV, before resuming photographic and bombing missions over Germany. It was 105 Squadron that made the first daylight attack by the RAF on Berlin, famously keeping Field Marshall Göring off the air during a planned radio speech.

The Mk IV Mosquito, as with several other variants, did not have any self-defence armament. The Mosquito was so fast that it could outfly many of its contemporaries, so the extra weight would not have been worth it.

'Thunder at Dawn' depicts a pair of de Havilland Mosquito Mk IVs flying low over the coast of Norfolk, where they were based during the Second World War. (Who knows how many other aircraft should be with them, but will never return?) The colours in this sort of image have to be spot on, or the finished result can be quite bizarre. In the sky for example, various shades of yellow, blending in with various shades of blue as one works the sky down from top to bottom, can result in an uncomfortable greeny colour (as yellow + blue = green). I use Cerulean Blue mixed with White and a very small amount of Burnt Sienna for the pale low down blue, blending in gently with Naples Yellow, Alizarin Crimson and White for the salmony horizon colour. The grasses were applied with a palette knife and really laid on thickly. This is always fun, as the result appears very quickly and helps to add to the depth in a painting as foreground features are always darker, more 'contrasty', and applied onto the canvas a lot more aggressively.

Oil on Canvas, in the collection of Dr Peter Stell

‘The Perfect Trainer’

de Havilland Tiger Moth

Work in progress

The image opposite illustrates an RAF training aircraft in its silver livery, certainly my favourite colour for an early aircraft type. It reminds me of my early days as a young boy building model aircraft, doping and painting the tissue covered balsawood frame with all the lovely smells and sounds of a sharp knife cutting the wood in just the right place.

I actually find painting silver doped fabric quite easy as it is basically grey paint with more white added for fabric exposed to light, and Payne’s grey added for fabric in shade. It can be very convincing, especially when the fabric is wrapped over a timber strip such as a wing rib, or fuselage stringer.

It is quite interesting to note that the painting is to all intents and purposes, a monotone canvas apart from the yellow bits. This can result in a very convincing effect supporting the adage, less is more.

The painting was a spontaneous speculative project, that was always going to be a simple canvas offering no challenges to the observer wondering what is supposed to be going on. I am a big believer in adding interest into an otherwise simple composition, in this case an aeroplane flying from right to left, but adding a dramatic sky to offer something extra for the observer to drink in.

It can often be misunderstood that the presence of dark gloomy looking clouds in a painting such as this represents a bad day. Not necessarily so. Dark gloomy looking clouds are only bright happy white clouds that happen to be in the shade of other clouds. It’s all the same stuff at the end of the day!

The original canvas was purchased at one of the Sandringham country shows in Norfolk. The lady who purchased it was an award winning model maker, so I know it has gone to a good home!

Sold at Sandringham show

'A Tiger's Tale'

de Havilland Tiger Moth

What more can be said about the beautiful little Tiger Moth that hasn't already been said? I do have a personal connection with it as a pilot. It wasn't the easiest machine to fly well, but for me this was one of the pleasures. I was truly flying an aeroplane in a proper pilot way! It did not take too much stretch of the imagination to become Biggles, but I must admit it was a good feeling to get down safely having dodged all those pesky bullets.

The Tiger was the first aeroplane for a great many trainee WWII pilots, as it was the primary trainer of the period. Inexperienced pilots, going through their training, loved the Moth with its rugged, tandem configuration, its sensitivity and 'Fighter Like' feel, unlike the aircraft that followed it…the Percival Prentice - big, chunky, with a side by side seating arrangement not popular with students as it resembled more of a classroom rather than a nimble fighter.

The painting 'A Tiger's Tale' depicts G-TIGA, based at the time of publication at Nottingham Airport, Tollerton. I enjoyed the process of producing this canvas as, on the day of visiting the aircraft, I was invited to fly it, bringing back many memories. TIGA was in the ownership of Derek Netherland at the time of visit, and he was the longest owner of a Tiger Moth, at over 30 years. It was said by a very observant viewer of the painting, that the far wing looked a little larger than the closer wing. He is actually quite correct, but this is due to there being an angle of stagger i.e. the wings are slightly swept back. The far wing is more of a true length while the close wing is slightly foreshortened.

The print shows Dick Flanagan, Chief Flying Instructor at Nottingham Airport Flying Club, discussing with my wife, how to avoid the ground anti-aircraft fire and dog fight techniques used by neighbouring flying clubs. My wife insisted on me painting her with long blonde hair. "No", she would say time and time again," I want it longer... No, still longer!" It took another three weeks to finish the painting.

Oil on Canvas

‘Night Fright, and Screaming Eagles Ready to Go’
Douglas C47 Skytrains

The Light Infantry division of the United States Army trained specifically to engage in air assault tasks. Their recognised operations during WWII included the D-Day Landings on the French coast, taking place on 6th June 1944. The Americans, unfortunately, suffered great losses on their designated beaches on the coast of Normandy.

Possibly the division’s most famous operation was during the Battle of the Bulge, engaging in heavy action near the city of Bastogne in Belgium during WWII.

My painting opposite shows a typical scene, during WWII, with Douglas C47 Skytrains ready to embark 101st airborne troops at RAF Membury.
The body of combat soldiers known as the 101st ‘Screaming Eagles’ was a light infantry division of the United States Army.

The closest aircraft shown was discovered in America, and purchased by its present owners, at one time having been on the waiting list to be scrapped. This was deemed unforgivable, as the aircraft was identified as being ‘Night Fright’, a C47 that actually operated from RAF Membury during the war. The airfield is directly next to Membury Estate, owned by the Walker family, responsible for discovering and restoring the aircraft to its original WWII status. Upon completion, the C47 will be flown back to Membury, where it will be based and flown from.

Producing the painting was in itself quite a task. Figure work is of paramount importance, getting the body language just right and not having people just standing straight up and literally doing nothing. I travelled down south, having organised a re-enactment group to pose for me. They also provided a Jeep, ammo boxes, guns etc. As far as composition is concerned, it is also very handy having more than one aircraft in the picture. The main subject sits nicely there, displaying all the attributes of the beautiful nose section and the nose art of course, a common thing attributed to the Americans, and important in this painting as it represents the very aeroplane that I was asked to paint. I decided to place a second aircraft in the painting, partly to add interest and partly to take advantage of the fact that I could literally place it anywhere to fill a blank space on the canvas.

The inset images illustrate the origination of a few of the subjects, and how they have been located in the composition to add interest and balance. Composition is so important when constructing a canvas. Note how, if the two main figure subjects had not been placed where they are, there would be a large area of plain concrete at the bottom of the canvas.

Oil on Canvas, in the collection of Mr Charlie Walker

‘Laarbruch Early Start’

English Electric Canberra B(I)8

The English Electric Canberra was the first Royal Air Force jet bomber to be put into service and became operational on 25th May 1951 and retired in 2006. Its first flight was in May 1949 so, at this time, there was still a lot to learn. The first jet engine was not developed until late in WWII. The Canberra was produced in high numbers during the 1950s and held the altitude world record of over 70,000ft. Due to its altitude capability and generally superior performance over and above the piston powered aircraft of the day, it was a very attractive purchase proposition for many air forces around the world.

The B(I)8 was introduced to fulfil the role of night- intruder bomber/interdictor, flying low-level missions in the European theatre. The special bomb bay doors allowed the B(I)8 Canberra to carry illumination flares that were used for night operations. Each wing had a bomb pod that was capable of carrying a 500 lb bomb or two 250 lb bombs. This gave the B(I)8 a sting in the tail used effectively by the Indian Air Force during their Congo operations in 1961. The type also had a nuclear capability and a photographic and electronic communication role. Designated as a bomber, the B(I)8 served only with the RAF’s Strike Squadrons in Germany.

The canvas depicts a 3 Squadron B(I)8 RAF Laarbruch, Germany, protected by the purpose built revetment, surrounded by the typical pine forest of the location. As the starter cartridges fire up, smoke is seen spilling out of the starter exhaust apertures. All this makes it a very attractive subject to paint, as it tells the observer that something is actually happening.

I made use of an accurate scale model to get the correct perspective and angle that I think yields the most advantageous view. The model was photographed from a distance of about 10ft and zoomed in to enlarge the image. If one were to photograph the model close up, the image would be subject to perspective error. In other words, the close wing would zoom out at the viewer, far too big, and the far wing would be tiny, an easy mistake to make.

Oil on Canvas, in the collection of Mr Adrian Thomas

‘The Last of the Biplanes’

Gloster Gladiator

One of my smaller, relatively inexpensive oils on canvas, this was painted whilst at the Duxford ‘Flying Legends 2009’ event. The actual aircraft was flying whilst it was being painted which I thought was rather nice. The image represents K7985 of 73 Squadron, presently based at the Shuttleworth Museum.

It was the last RAF biplane fighter. Although it was being rapidly overtaken from a technical point of view by aircraft of increased armament and speed, the beautiful little biplane stood its ground and kept fighting into WWII alongside Hurricanes and Spitfires. Overseas air forces were taking advantage of the fighting attributes of the Gladiator during the 1930s. Progress from an engineering point of view moved forward at an incredible rate at this point in history, so it was known for quite a long time that aircraft of a higher spec. would come off the drawing board at a high rate, but having said that, the Gladiator was the first biplane to sport an enclosed canopy.

It can be seen at a glance that the Gladiator was a development of the Gloster Gauntlet to a ministry specification that would see the Gauntlet’s follow up design have higher speed and heavier armament. The Gladiator would see the speed increased to 250mph with armament of four machine guns.

I had to paint the Gladiator simply because, to me, the construction of the Gladiator literally makes it a huge model aeroplane with fuselage stringer construction, enclosed in silver doped canvas - in itself a lovely effect to catch in oils. Helping to catch the effect of distance in the painting, you will notice how the hedge lines in the fields get closer and more compacted the higher up and closer to the horizon they get, similar to the cloud effect in ‘Preparing for Action’. These are the tools available to the artist.

Oil on Canvas

‘Hatilen Ronteriios. (Warriors of the Air)’

Handley Page Halifax

The Handley Page Halifax was a large four-engined RAF bomber operated during WWII. Its first flight was 25th October 1939, and it was introduced into the RAF on 13th November 1940. Other operators of the type were the Royal Canadian Air Force, the Royal Australian Air Force, and the Free French Air Force.

This ‘Halibag’ (as it was affectionately known) of 431 Squadron RCAF is seen over the north coast of the Flamborough Peninsula, returning to its base airfield at Croft, after a mission over enemy lines. It is flying in formation with a Wellington of the same squadron.

The Wellington was in fact 431 Squadron’s first aircraft until converting over to Halifax Vs. It was equipped with Vs until April 1944, after which it went over to Halifax IIIs which had more powerful Bristol Hercules radial engines in place of the older Rolls Royce Merlins. The number sequence sounds wrong but is actually correct.

The painting represents a typical aerial scenario with a significant presence of both cloud and ground, always a good excuse to show depth and distance on a flat canvas. In this particular case note the relatively pale, soft tones of the ground compared to the airframe. As distance increases, there obviously is more atmosphere to look through with all its pollution, i.e. dust etc, consequently, the image you are looking at is paler, with softer colours. A classic example of this is looking at several cars in the distance. If far enough away, a group of different coloured cars (red, blue etc.) will all take on a pale grey/blue tint.

It is interesting to note that most of the beautiful orange and salmon colours in those romantic atmospheric sunsets and sunrises are due mostly to the pollution in the atmosphere. Don’t worry…although the expression atmospheric pollution in this modern world is associated with human intervention, most is, in fact, natural dust and foreign particles not associated with our presence. I adore the constantly changing appearance of the sky, and love painting it, which is quite lucky for me actually as aeroplanes spend a lot of time in it. My daughter makes fun of me in commercial aircraft as my head is constantly twisted at 90 degrees taking in the beauty of the skyscape.

The painting was a commission and now hangs in the collection of Mr Marc Hill.

Oil on Canvas, in the collection of Mr Marc Hill

'One Way Ticket'
Hawker Hurricane

In order to protect the Atlantic convoy ships during WWII from the long range German bombers, the Condors, it was necessary to take Hawker Hurricanes along with them, mounted on a rocket-powered catapult assembled on the bow of several of the merchant ships. When there was a threat from the enemy, the Hurricane was launched to attack or ward off the enemy, and then ditched in the sea. The initial brief was for the pilot to attempt to ditch in the sea as close as possible to the nearest ship, but the effect of the large radiator underneath the fuselage was to tip the aircraft over, putting the pilot's life at even more risk. A new tactic was drawn up, recommending the pilot climb to a sufficient altitude and bale out. This did represent, in itself, a dangerous situation, as it was less likely the pilot would find himself close enough to a ship for a convenient rescue.

Interestingly, the rocket rail was set at an angle to the centreline of the ship to ensure the Hurricane was not run over by the ship if the launch failed. Launching was a tricky procedure. There was a time delay between the fire officer pressing the go button and the Hurricane leaving the end of the ramp. Hurricanes were, of course, rapidly becoming technically overtaken by the Spitfire at this stage of the war and were in fact becoming quite disposable.

An irresistible subject for me to paint, I couldn't ask for more - moody sky, sea, ship and aircraft. For me, the rougher the sea the better. The inspiration for the painting originated from a documentary on television showing a large merchantman heaving almost out of control on the high seas. It reminded me of my time at sea in the Royal Navy, and I knew there and then it had to be caught in oils on canvas. The concept of the 'Hurri Cat' (Hurricane catapult) was familiar to me, so done deal, this was to be my next painting.

Oil on Canvas

'Letters From Home'

Hawker Hurricane

Painted as a commission, the image reflects the all too rare moment of relaxation for the aircrew on a fighter base during WWII. The aircraft featured, of course, is that of Bob Stanford Tuck of 257 Squadron, based at RAF Coltishall. Tuck was a highly decorated fighter pilot during his fighter career with DSO, DFC and two bars. Tuck joined the RAF in 1935 and first engaged in combat during the Battle of France. Tuck's first taste of victory was on 23rd May 1940 when he actually shot down three German fighters, the next day adding to his score with the shooting down of two bombers. On 28th January 1942 Tuck was shot down by anti-aircraft fire and taken prisoner. At the time of his capture, he had shot down twenty-seven enemy aircraft.

I had some help from a re-enactment group. A photo on this page shows one of the chaps walking away from me, not posing, just walking away as if I was not there. This is the secret when taking advantage of re-enactors, just invite them to get on with their day as they would in their period role, and just click away.

I like airframes that are grubby and battle scarred. Aircraft that look like proper war birds and not full sized plastic kits. I have to admit, if I was in charge of a rebuild to flying condition project of something like a Hurricane, I would enhance cordite/oil/exhaust heat stains. I would break through the red-doped gun patches (blanked-off holes of course) as though they had been fired and chip away paint on panel lines that the engineers and armourers had created during their work. Just me, I suppose it is the artist coming out in me.

Oil on Canvas, in the collection of Dr Peter Stell

'We Never Slept'
Hawker Hurricanes

The Hawker Hurricane, was, without doubt, the most numerous RAF aircraft to fly in the Battle of Britain. Few people who have a passing interest in the Battle's history realise that the Hurricane actually shot down twice as many enemy aircraft as did the Spitfire. The Hurricane was built in a traditional way, using wood and doped fabric, as opposed to the concept of monocoque construction. The Spitfire was built with monocoque aluminium construction, the principle being that the strength of the airframe was taken up by, and relied upon, the aluminium skin of the fuselage, rather like the shell of an egg. The main disadvantage of this construction principle was that, as with an egg, if a small part of the skin was breached, the overall strength of the fuselage was impaired, rendering the aircraft vulnerable to further damage.

So, the Hurricane was a tough little aeroplane that could take a great deal of punishment. After sustaining damage in combat, fabric could be seen flapping about all over the place, revealing the wooden stringer construction, but the little fighter would fight on. There was indeed, quite a long period of time during WWII that the Hurricane was in full RAF service alongside the Spitfire.

The Hurricane had to survive within the realms of the RAF in the presence of the Spitfire with one main disadvantage that was to be its downfall. Due to its traditional 'chunky' tough construction as described, the wing inevitably had to be very thick. This meant that the top speed was limited, and an inappropriate amount of power increase would be necessary to increase effectively the top speed of the aircraft. So, in the presence of the Spitfire, the Hurricane's days were numbered.

The image opposite shows aircraft of 605 Squadron RAF in 1940. The motto of 605 Squadron is 'We Never Slept' hence the composition and title of the painting. UP-W was piloted by Plt Off Bob Foster DFC during the battle. UP-W is the oldest surviving flying Hurricane from the Battle of Britain. My painting raised £4,500 at an RAF charity auction in London. How could I want a better job than this!

Oil on Canvas, auctioned in aid of the Battle of Britain Trust

‘Another Dawn’

Hawker Typhoon

Designed to supersede the Spitfire and Hurricane, the Typhoon was specifically intended to be faster and carry heavier armament to satisfy the Air Ministry’s demand for a more effective attack aircraft. The Typhoon was conceived by the aircraft designer Sydney Camm.

The Typhoon was powered by the first engine to have the dubious honour of being the first unit to weigh in at one ton, nicknamed the ‘One Ton Monster’. Initially, due to it’s complex use of sleeve valves and severe cooling problems the Sabre suffered from mechanical failures. The Sabre was the ultimate engine from Napier’s innovative “H” configuration series engines, tracing it’s roots through their Rapier and Dagger powerplants. It was eventually developed to produce 3500hp, essentially two Horizontally Opposed engines joined to make a powerful compact engine.

The Typhoon depicted, PR-G R7752, was the mount of Sqn Ldr Roland Beamont, the Commanding Officer of 609 Squadron, CBE, DSO and bar, DFC.

The painting was a commission, with the sky being used from a photograph taken by the person who commissioned the painting, from the flight deck of his airliner. I love the mystical, almost romantic atmosphere of morning and evening skies, with the enchanting beauty of the salmon pink under-bellies of the clouds just catching the colour of the sun at that time of day.

The small Typhoon image on this page also represents a Typhoon from 609 Squadron and was actually a miniature canvas measuring approximately 6in x 4in. I find my miniatures are very popular as they are a reasonably priced introduction into the world of purchasing original art work, and do make a nice collection if grouped closely with each other, possibly collected over a period of time.

The original painting ‘Another Dawn’ was commissioned by, and now hangs in the collection of, Captain Darryl Elliott

Oil on Canvas, in the collection of Captain Darryl Elliott

‘Falklands Freedom’

Lockheed C-130 Hercules

The Hercules is a mainstay workhorse for mainly the Royal Air Force, United States Air Force, United States Marine Corps and the Royal Canadian Air Force. Originally built by Lockheed, latterly Lockheed Martin, the Hercules is a four-engined turboprop military transport aircraft. It certainly has a long service history. In 2007 the Hercules had spent fifty years of continuous service in the hands of its original operator, the United States Air Force, surviving a continuous production run of sixty years to date, an all-time record. The aircraft has been so successful as a basic airframe it has manifested itself through several variants and modifications to the eventual Hercules of today, 2016, the Lockheed Martin C-130J Super Hercules, sporting upgraded engines, flight deck and electronic systems. It is such a popular aircraft that over 300 C-130Js have been delivered to more than a dozen air forces to date.

During the period after the Falklands conflict a substantial British Service presence was established and maintained in the area. Part of this, of course, was the RAF. The image depicts a Hercules of 1312 Flight during one of their training exercises in the Falklands. The object of this exercise was to train fighter pilots to detect, home in to, and destroy, enemy aircraft under the most extreme conditions. It was also an opportunity for the Hercules pilots to hone their evasion skills using the cover of the cliffs. This meant flying at low levels in adverse conditions.

One of the challenges of tackling such a painting, is creating a situation where one can tell the identity of an aircraft type even though it is quite a long way away and small on the painting. Such is the case here, where there is a Phantom chasing the Hercules. For this purpose, it was necessary to construct and study a model of the Phantom, even though it was relatively small on the canvas.

The original painting was commissioned by, and now hangs in the collection of, Captain Nick Stein. Nick actually flew in the depicted aircraft and gave me a great deal of help, adding to the pleasure it was to paint for him. The image illustrates Nick’s aircraft at the time of his RAF service in the Falklands in 1986.

Oil on Canvas, in the collection of Captain Nick Stein

‘The Tail Chase.’

Supermarine Spitfire/Messerschmitt Bf 109

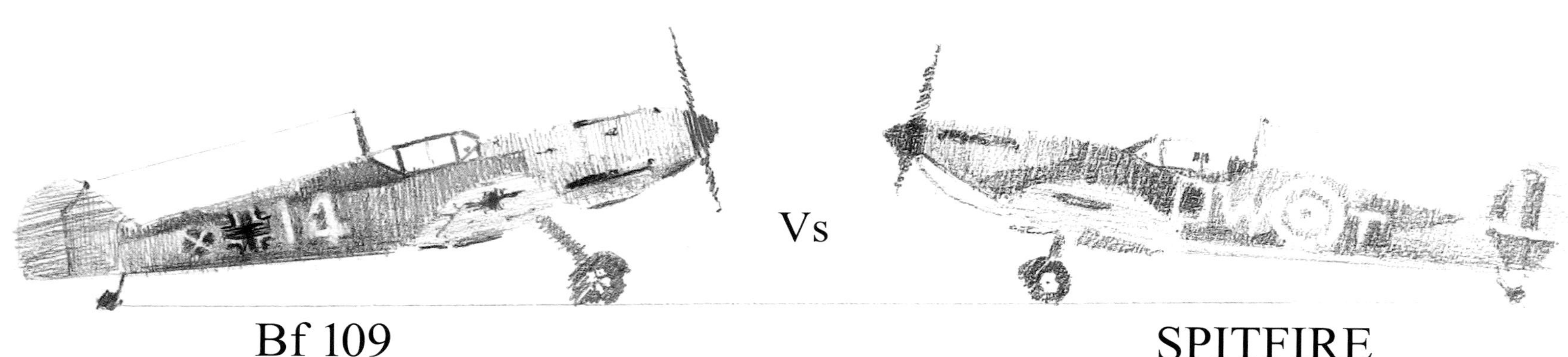

Actual air combat scenarios have never (unless on a commission basis) been a priority with me. As can be seen from much of the content of this book, I do appreciate the challenge of depicting aircraft on the ground, sitting there contentedly like a wild animal in its natural environment waiting to pounce.

Every now and again I do, however, feel the need to express a little action and movement. My painting ‘The Tail Chase’ depicts a typical south coast encounter during the Battle of Britain. The encounter, as can be seen, is in the location of Beachy Head, a site that guaranteed a good viewing of the Battle action during the summer of 1940. Of course, we don’t know if the Spitfire got the better of the German Bf 109, but it is quite possible that the enemy did get away from the Supermarine Spitfire. The two adversaries during certain periods of time during WWII were comparable, with the outcome of victory of one over the other indeed depending on the personal skills and experience of the individual pilots.

One clear technical advantage of the Bf 109 over the Spitfire (and Hurricane) during the Battle of Britain was the fact that the Messerschmitt pilot could escape from the British fighters by pushing the nose down into a steep dive, sustaining negative ’G’ without the engine cutting out from fuel starvation as it had direct fuel injection. The Rolls Royce Merlin engine had a carburettor which meant that to follow the Messerschmitt, the Spitfire pilot had to roll inverted and pull back on the stick, thereby maintaining positive ‘G’ throughout the manoeuvre. This disadvantage was partially resolved in late 1940 by a device called ‘Miss Shilling’s Orifice’ (invented by a young female engineer at RAE Farnborough called Beatrice Shilling). Officially known as the RAE Restrictor, this simple solution sufficed until 1943 when the Bendix Rolls Royce pressure carburettor was introduced which kept positive fuel pressure to the Merlin during all negative G manoeuvres.

As with a lot of my compositions, the canvas relied on my experience of landscape painting, as well as knowledge of aircraft - this example containing not only the inevitable skyscape, but sea as well as the hard landscape of rocks and grass. As an artist, it is important to generate a pleasing design that benefits from good balance. In this particular case, the main subject, the Bf 109, is certainly not in the middle of the canvas, but is balanced by the inclusion of the cliffs on the left and the Spitfire quite high up making sure the interest is not too low down on the canvas.

Oil on Canvas, in the collection of Dr Peter Stell

‘Mitsubishi A6M Zero’

One of the major factors that made the Zero so strong and manoeuvrable was the principle of manufacture, discovered by the Americans upon inspecting a ditched aircraft. Described as an airframe made to incredibly high standards of precision, the Zero was considerably lighter than American contemporaries, largely due to the wing being made in one piece, as opposed to two wings joined together. The airframe rivets were flush, which made the aircraft slip much more efficiently through the air. All in all, a very profitable find.

The image, depicts a Zero after ditching in the shallow waters just off the Solomon Islands in the South Pacific. Ditched aircraft such as this one offer a wonderful habitat for sub aqua wildlife and are very soon taken over by all sorts of beautiful coral and strange looking fish. Nowadays aircraft wrecks are in fact intentionally lowered down into the warm waters at suitable locations for the very purpose of wildlife colonisation.

One thing that attracts me to this sort of composition is the wonderful shade of blue that is found at that depth. Just 30ft down it is another world. There is always an opportunity to play with light in this sort of composition. On the propeller, there is a deposition of growth that cries out for tiny shadows, so subtle, but it can be simple details like this that attract a lot of attention.

Oil on Canvas, in the collection of Mr Andrew North

‘Tornado Alley’

Panavia Tornado GR4

The Tornado is a supersonic swing wing fighter aircraft designed and developed by Panavia, a multi country consortium consisting of the United Kingdom, West Germany and Italy. The variable-geometry wing allows the aircraft to operate at maximum operating efficiency depending on what is being asked of the aircraft i.e. taking off, landing, cruising or fighting.

There are three variants in the Tornado family, the IDS (Interdictor Strike), ECR (Electronic Combat Reconnaissance) and ADV (Air Defence Variant).

The type first flew on 14th August 1974 but did not enter service until 1979/80. The only other country to adopt the Tornado apart from the three consortium nations was the Royal Saudi Air Force. Production continued until 1998 resulting in a total of 992 being built.

The Tornado is cleared to carry the majority of air-launched weapons in the NATO inventory, including various unguided and laser-guided bombs, anti-ship and anti-radiation missiles, as well as specialised weapons such as anti-personnel mines and anti-runway munitions. The painting opposite, depicts a Tornado carrying a typical ordnance package at high speed low level.

I was drawn to the idea of catching a fast jet at low level after spending a week in the Lake District during a very good period of weather. I have since seen many photographs of jets flying at low level, but usually from a vantage point that is accessible and well known to the public. I wanted to show the aircraft with a slightly less familiar background. I also wanted to depict the scenario as if one is flying in close formation with the aircraft. This obviously would not have been a credible situation in real life, but represents a well-used technique in the world of aviation art.

I resisted the temptation to blur the background even though the aircraft is travelling at a fair speed. With the ground being approximately half a mile away and the jet not travelling directly from right to left, (slightly out of the canvas) the ground would in fact not be moving across the line of sight very fast, consequently not yielding a blurred effect. I have seen paintings where the background has been unnecessarily blurred, and to me, this often spoils the finished result.

As a guide to deciding what the best angle to view the aircraft would be, I built a level 5 plastic kit, (not for the beginner). It was well worth doing as it allowed me to become quite familiar with the design of the airframe. It was a very sophisticated model and was a challenge to build.

Oil on Canvas, at time of publication, still for sale

‘Schedule Disrupted’

Royal Aircraft Factory BE2c

The RAF (or Royal Aircraft Factory) BE2c served with the Royal Flying Corps from 1914 until 1919. It was an agile little aeroplane that served well in its duty as a fighting aircraft within the RFC. It was kept in front line use during a period of time after it became obsolete. This was due to difficulty in finding a suitable replacement for it. Operational duties included reconnaissance, artillery spotting, light bombing, night fighting and ultimately, training and communications. Incredibly, over 3,500 of these flimsy aircraft were built in a little over five years.

In the early days of aviation, it was often the case that many firms built under licence a certain type of aircraft, and this was indeed the case of the BE2c. Companies that had not been heard of by the general public often were involved in the construction process. The design of the type had an inherently stable characteristic in flight, allowing the crew to go about their duties unhindered, these being mainly reconnaissance and photography in early years. The BE2c followed on from the BE2b with a new fuselage, more wing dihedral (the angle the wings bow up when viewed from the front) and including the use of ailerons instead of wing warping (twisting) as was the case with all very early types. Ailerons are the small flaps on the trailing edge of the wings, the left one going up whilst the right aileron goes down (or vice versa). The effect of this is to tilt the aircraft left or right as part of turning. It always amazes me how long it took the designers and engineers to realise how beneficial this principle was, as opposed to forcibly twisting the whole wing. I think maybe the relationship between bird flight and the ‘New Flying Machine’ was still at that point in time very close and took some time to break away from.

The BE2c painting opposite was commissioned by the WWI aviation magazine ‘Cross and Cockade’ for the cover illustration of their members’ publication. It shows BE2c 4301 on 25th September 1915, piloted by 2Lt J N C Washington, with observer 2Lt M W Greenhow, attacking Douai-Valenciennes rail yard in France. They are in trouble, as the German Fokker Eindecker monoplane fighters were soon on the scene.

Oil on Canvas, commissioned by Cross and Cockade for their magazine cover

‘Fees to the Front’

Royal Aircraft Factory FE2b

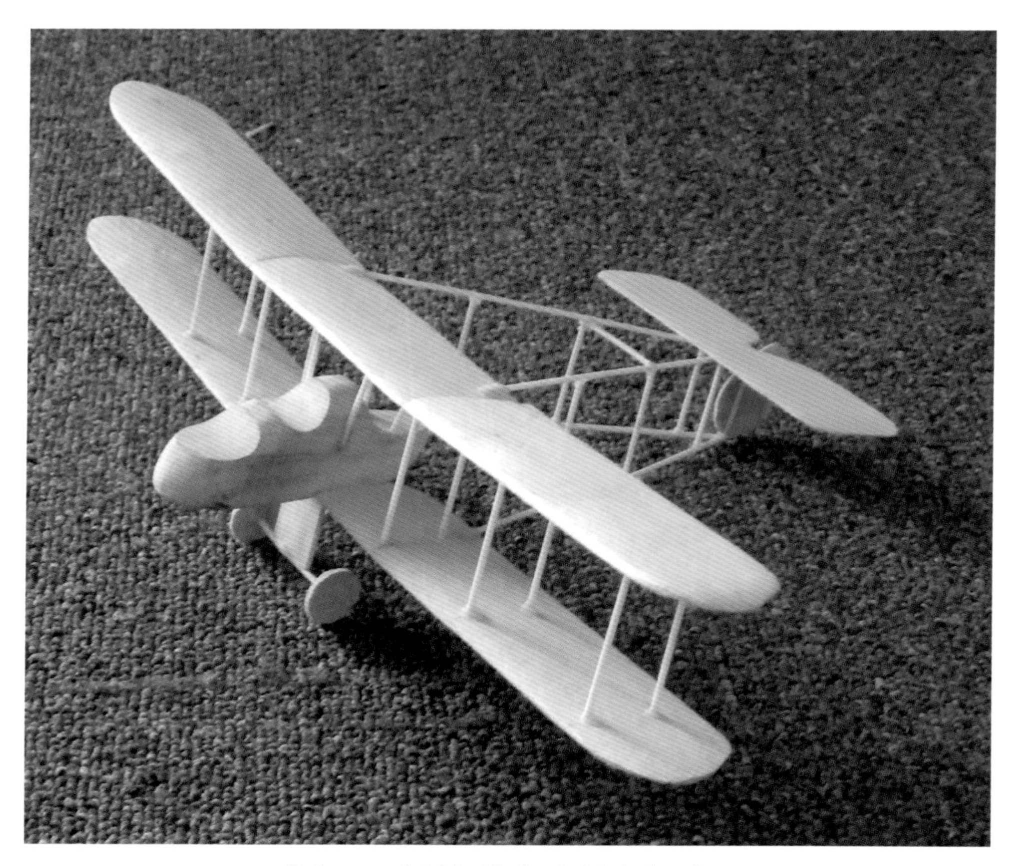

Balsa model I built for initial sketches

This painting was commissioned by film director Sir Peter Jackson, a true WWI aviation fan. Peter has in fact built two FE2bs to flying status from scratch. They are fabulous reproductions, sporting original Beardmore engines, having been re-built using original drawings.

To me, with a working knowledge of aerodynamics, if there had been a competition to design a flying machine with the least aerodynamic efficiency, the FE2b would have won. It appears that, so long as the machine lifted off the ground in some manner and was capable of carrying a gun, job done. To be honest, I have so much admiration for everybody involved in this pioneering aviation adventure with so much still to learn, from basic flight handling, to managing the aeroplane in combat situations. Compared to today, aircraft fell out of the sky at relatively frequent intervals, due to anything from early engineering aircraft stresses, to lack of flying experience for new pilots.

Manufactured by the Royal Aircraft Factory, the FE2b was used as a Fighter Reconnaissance/Night bomber, FE standing for Farman Experimental. The type was a two-seater with pilot in the back and gunner/observer in the front. The fighter entered service towards the end of 1915, arriving at the Western Front in January 1916 as a front line fighter. It was around this time that aircraft were designated fighters on the drawing board right from the start, rather than just fitting guns on to existing aircraft. The pusher configuration lent itself perfectly to the forward firing gun as there was no propeller to obscure the firing line. The pusher types were superseded quite quickly due to the invention of an interrupter gear. Quite simply, when a prop blade went in front of the gun barrel, the gun didn’t fire. This secured the interrupter fitted aircraft as a true fighting machine.

Oil on Canvas, in the collection of Sir Peter Jackson

'Early Morning Preparations'

Royal Aircraft Factory RE8

The painting was commissioned by film director Sir Peter Jackson for his art collection. The RE8 (Reconnaissance Experimental 8) is one of the aircraft types in his WWI aviation museum. The RE8 was a two-seat reconnaissance bomber, first flight 17th June 1916, designed and built to replace the obsolete BE2. Advancements in airframe construction and basic design were still slow at that period of time, and left the RE8 not being the superior aircraft it was supposed to be, with a reputation of being not the easiest aeroplane to fly. The RE8 did, however, survive in military service as the standard reconnaissance/spotter aircraft through to the end of the war, fighting in many more theatres than the Western Front, including Italy and Russia. There were certainly plenty to go round, as over 4,000 were produced.

The installation of the Royal Aircraft Factory 4a air-cooled engine of 150 hp and V12 cylinder configuration gave the RE8 a distinctive appearance similar to the preceding BE 12 with the vertical exhausts and large air intake. This prominent air intake actually directed the air right back to the rear cylinder, making sure it received as much cooling air as the ones at the front. It is often mistaken for a carburettor air intake.

A trip to Duxford gave me the necessary detail information to progress with the painting, and a ground scenario was to be the final composition. The museum's RE8 is hanging from the ceiling at Duxford in the Airspace Exhibition Hall. In the painting I have taken advantage of the often rough and ready ground conditions that were prevalent during the First World War and used this to add interest to the canvas. As anticipated, this did bring to bear my landscape skills, and, when one looks at all the sky, background hills and trees, water, fence posts, buildings etc, one can appreciate there is more to being an aviation artist than just painting aircraft. I like to include people in my paintings, especially when uniforms and classic working clothes of the period are involved. I travelled to meet a re-enactment group to have them pose for me, and was delighted to see a black leather coat in front of me. One of the advantages of having human figures in a painting is that the artist can literally place them on the canvas wherever he or she wants, in order to balance the composition nicely.

One of the things I find satisfying when painting something like a WWI aircraft, is catching in paint the way it was actually built. All that stitched canvas, with the associated cording passing through reinforced holes pulling the material into all sorts of interesting shapes, with dints and creases all over the place just crying out to be caught in paint.

Oil on Canvas, in the collection of Sir Peter Jackson

‘Sikorsky MH-53 Pave Low’

The Sikorsky MH-53 Pave Low is a heavy long-range combat search and rescue helicopter in service with the United States Air Force. The type does have development history, as it was an upgrade from the HH-53B/C Sikorsky Sea Stallion. Nicknamed the ‘Super Jolly Green Giant’, the helicopter eventually joined in with special operations, taking advantage of its versatile capability, along with its advanced technological status and transport capacity.

The MH-53’s terrain following capability was better than anything else operational at the time. The pilot of the subject helicopter, Chuck Gutshall, informed me that Pave Low stands for ‘Precision Avionics Vector Equipment Low Obstacle Warning’.

I met Chuck at RAF Cosford, in the aviation museum where the Pave Low helicopter is exhibited. He showed me around the machine and introduced me to the .50 calibre rapid fire M2 Browning machine gun pointing out of the back, a very frightening piece of kit, but very useful when picking up Special Ops Soldiers, one of the helicopter’s specific operational duties.

General spec.-
Crew: Six (Two Pilots, Two Flight Engineers and Two Aerial Gunners)
Capacity: Thirty-seven troops
Empty weight: 32,000lb
Max. takeoff weight: 46,000lb (50,000lb combat weight)
Powerplant: Two × T64-GE-100 turboshaft, 4,330 shp
Performance Maximum speed: 170 knots (196 mph)

Oil on Canvas, hanging in the collection of Chuck Gutshall

‘Pups at Play’
Sopwith Pups

During the First World War, because aviation was in its pioneering stage and designs were still experimental, flying machines often had their own unique handling characteristics which could challenge the pilot. The Sopwith Pup was an exception because its handling was so sweet and was a machine that pilots truly loved to fly compared to its successor, the Sopwith Camel, which was a bit of a handful and killed more pilots through handling accidents than the Pup.The Pup was far more stable and compared to the Camel, a pleasure to fly.

The Pup was a well-loved fighting machine, sporting the device that increased the efficiency of the aircraft as a fighter…the gun forward firing interrupter device.

Skies are so important to me in any sort of composition, whether it be a landscape or an aviation painting. I try to give the impression of actually being in the sky, and in this particular case I have concentrated on sculpturing the cloudscape to have foreground, middleground, and background, with the peak of the middleground cloud extending above the horizon line.

My painting depicts two Pups in this sky having a bit of fun during a quiet spell in the hostilities.

Oil on Canvas

'All the King's Men'

Still Life

It quite surprises people when I tell them that this is one of my favourite paintings. I adore still life. I love the design process; knowing, from a visual point of view, everything is totally under your control right from the start. Putting this here, draping that there, folding this in just the right manner. I like it when items are not new, i.e. worn leather, damaged map etc. The purchaser of the painting did come back to me pointing out that the canvas was damaged at a certain place. I had the pleasure of pointing out to him that it was the painted image of the worn map.

The original idea was to have the kit (that I borrowed from a 'kit collector' friend) scattered about in an artistic way over the radio desk in a Lancaster. I was invited to go on board 'Just Jane' the taxiing Lancaster at East Kirkby to see what could be organised. I placed the kit on the radio table and could see immediately that the composition was far too complex and confusing with all the controls, dials and switches. It had to be simplified somehow. I arrived back home and deposited the gear on our writing table. Lo and behold, that was it. In one unexpected stroke I solved the problem. All I needed to do was go round to my mother in law, pick up her old ration book, my father in law's pipe, and one or two other items.

Oil on Canvas, in the collection of Captain Andrew, and Mrs. Geraldine Dixon

I borrowed an old WWII aviation map that sat in the composition beautifully. It offered a splash of light and a nice surface to allow shadows to be cast over it. I had to really force a bend in it to allow it to hang over the edge. Along with the map, came a period copy of 'The Daily Telegraph'. This sat with the map nicely and enhanced the area of light spread over the desk top.

One thing I did learn about the map during the painting of this canvas, was that the navigators would highlight, in dark blue, all of the rail lines. There were so many rail routes across the country in those days that they were of great use to navigators map reading their way around the whole country. The limited edition print of the painting has been out for a while now, so I will reveal what used to be a well-kept secret. In the text of the newspaper, hidden somewhere in the small writing, it says, "I love Cas" (my wife).

I couldn't resist the temptation to paint a still life celebrating the achievements of Sydney Camm, the designer of the Hawker Hurricane, and of many other well known types including the Hawker Fury/Hart/Demon etc. I enjoyed a visit to Brooklands, the home of pioneering aviation and, of course, the Brooklands aviation archives, where I was very honoured to gain access to many of the items within the composition of the painting. As one can imagine, rendering the blue print was a very rewarding challenging NIGHTM

Oil on Canvas

‘Speak Merlin!’

Supermarine Spitfire

The concept for my painting ‘Speak Merlin!’ was inspired by a journey in my car travelling past a scene where a farmer was stubble burning in a crop field. Early Spitfire marques were flying well before stubble burning was banned during WWII, so I couldn’t resist depicting a cheeky stolen moment of fun as a pilot flies low over an appreciative group of farm workers.

It is often said that the best view of the Spitfire is a top-ish view, revealing the crescent shaped wings, the signature design feature of the Spitfire. I actually love the Spit from other angles. I have always liked the bubble canopy and the shape of the cowl chin. The cowl bulging out for the exhaust stubs flattening the top of the cowling, all adds to the perfect design of the Spitfire airframe. I chose a near head-on angle to build up a composition for the scenario. I do not think it is always necessary to take a three quarter front or back view for a good action painting. The chosen view enhances the illusion of depth by flying the Spitfire from deep inside the canvas to practically overhead as it zooms out of the canvas, hence the title ‘Speak Merlin!’ The sound of that Merlin engine will ring in the farmer’s ears for some time to come.

Considered by many to be one of the most successful internal combustion aero engines ever, the Merlin was a 27 litre capacity 12 cylinder Vee configured engine. Its first test run was in 1933. Rolls Royce named their piston aero engines after birds of prey. It was indeed so successful that most of the significant aircraft operated by the RAF during the war were powered by Merlin engines....Spitfire / Hurricane/Lancaster/Mosquito and Halifax being just some of the best known.

The painting was a speculative canvas giving me the opportunity to let myself go, so to speak. All artists have their own style and techniques. One of my considerations, when composing a canvas, is never to consider it of importance to have the main subject occupying too much space in the painting. Simply, don’t make the aeroplane too big. In my painting ‘Speak Merlin!’ I have enjoyed the landscape to the point where one’s eye roams around the canvas picking up the atmosphere, and hopefully, in one’s imagination, waiting for the roar of that wonderful, perfect Merlin engine.

Oil on Canvas

‘The Cold War 1941’

Supermarine Spitfires

The image shows Spitfires of 317 (Polish) Squadron being prepared for another day on standby. The featured aircraft is JH-C. This particular aircraft can still be seen flying at Duxford during the airshows throughout the year. The interesting vehicle is in fact a six cylinder Bedford glycol/water bowser. I found it an irresistible temptation to include this in the composition when the guys at East Kirkby offered to wheel it out of the museum hangar for me.

The painting was a commission. Part of the brief was to include a fence running across the foreground but I do feel the image benefited from a well-dilapidated old fence, allowing the viewer to walk into the scene.

317 Squadron was one of 16 Polish fighter Squadrons in the RAF during the Second World War. Polish Squadrons made a tremendous impact on the war, particularly during the Battle of Britain, resulting in a Polish Squadron achieving the highest kill score rate. This was 303 Squadron, with a total kill score of 126 for the Battle of Britain alone. 317 Squadron achieved forty eight kills during WWII.

The ground crew, as seen in the image, suffered terribly during the winters of the war, with often nothing more than makeshift shelters to protect them from the savage elements.

One comment from an observer questioned the proportion of the ground crew member at the nose of the Spit. My reply was to draw to the gentleman’s attention the fact that the diameter of the prop is about 11ft so the length of the single blade pointing down is 5ft 6in. Compare the length of the blade with the height of the man and I personally would suggest the guy is about right. I make mention of this as I hope you may find it of interest to see what aids and clues there are available to the artist.

Oil on Canvas, in the collection of Mr and Mrs Peter Hamilton

'Pulling Together'

It can sometimes be forgotten just how much combined effort was required to put together a fighting force that would stop Adolf Hitler in his tracks. It was not only the revered and celebrated efforts and sacrifices of the pilots and associated aircrews, but the background heroes that, as a result of their efforts, got and kept them in the air, flying reliable, well-armed and serviced aircraft. It was a priority, of course, to ensure the aircrew and the equally important ground crew were fit and healthy. It was the job of the forgotten 'Women's Land Army' to help fill a void and keep our boys fed.

It was also a challenge to ensure the morale of the nation's population was high, and kept high, in such adverse conditions during the war. One of the most demoralising conditions of a theatre of war is hunger. In June 1939 it was the food requirement that initiated the organization known as the WLA, or Women's Land Army, to recruit girls on to the land to replace the men that went to war. The farmers of the land were their employers. Approximately a third of the Land Army came from London, but most of the remainder came from the larger towns and cities around England.

The painting sees a pair of Spitfires that have survived a dogfight over the English Channel flying appreciatively over a group of waving Land Army girls.

Although the painting is more leaning towards landscape than aviation, accuracy was still of paramount importance. From a historic point of view, the cart is known as a Sussex Cart, and has its own particular characteristics. Body colour has to be dark blue and wheels have to be red. The front wheel has to have twelve spokes, the rear fourteen spokes and so it goes on….The horsey bit was great. Carol and I visited a Heavy Horse Centre in Lincolnshire and were given free access to study the beautiful creature named William. The detail in the harness and brass regalia was fascinating and I couldn't wait to put brush to canvas.

Towards the end of the day, we did have a near death experience! We were contentedly having a cup of tea on a bench seat, when we noticed a heavy horse hurtling out of control straight towards us. "DON'T MOVE!" was heard shouted from a distance. I seem to remember the only part of me that did actually move was my right hand scribing a crucifix across my chest, oh and I think my top lip quivered a little, like just before you start to cry.

With Carol, I visited a Land Army re-enactor's home to get good accurate figure work references. Carol was invited to get dressed in Land Army uniform as well, and is actually the figure at the front with the stick in her hand. After questioning its loose fit, Carol was told that in the war there were only two sizes of kit, too large or too small.

Oil on Canvas, sold at the Guild of Aviation Artists Annual Exhibition, Mall Galleries, London

‘Seek and Destroy’
Supermarine Spitfires

On 26th July 1940, 41 Squadron flew into RAF Hornchurch, one of the Sector Stations serving 11 Group in the south east of England. Operating from this station, they saw their first action in the early stages of the Battle of Britain. On the 5th September the Squadron experienced the worst day in its history. The Commanding Officer and OC of B Flight were both killed with three other pilots shot down, with a further two pilots wounded. On 31st October 1940 the Battle of Britain was officially over. Forty-nine pilots flew with the Squadron from the 10th July - 31st October, but the losses must never be forgotten. Ten were killed and twelve wounded. This painting’s title is the 41 Squadron motto in their honour.

‘Seek and Destroy’ represents a flight of Spitfires from 41 Squadron during the Battle of Britain. The painting started out life in a rather peculiar way. It actually started as a grey foreboding sky, with me wondering what to put in it. I took the sky reference with my camera on a rather dull day from my cottage in Derby. I zoomed in with my telephoto lens on a section of sky that I thought would be appropriate for a future painting. As part of painting the sky, I darkened down a small area in the bottom left corner and added evidence of a river. This gives the impression of one being in the sky looking down rather than on the ground looking up, as I was, of course.

I never copy photographs directly, and love composing my paintings in a manner that I would ideally like to see them. In this case, my intention was to have in line abreast a flight of six Spitfires but making sure they do not present themselves in a perfect straight line. To assist with the the composition, I made use of an accurate scale model, sitting it on the end of a piece of wire and photographing it. Keeping the camera in the same position, I then moved the model a little further away, raised it a tad and a bit forward, tilted the wings a bit then photographed it again. This high tech method was continued until there was the quantity of aircraft that I wanted.

Oil on Canvas

‘Merlins in the Mist’

Supermarine Spitfires 616 Squadron

One could earn a living painting and sketching the Supermarine Spitfire only. I enjoy the task of trying to discover novel ways of producing an image that generates interest and excitement, even though it might be the familiar and well painted Spitfire.

I have seen and admired many paintings of aircraft in beautiful misty, atmospheric sunrises and sunsets, but very rarely in thick fog. If there is one thing that I love about catching mood in a painting, it is the illusion of depth and distance. In my Spitfire painting opposite, I composed my scenario to reflect this illusion, hopefully to best advantage. There is, of course, the adage within the world of creative crafts, ‘less is more’, and I designed my canvas around this principle. There is no detail on the horizon line. There is no character in the sky, just the evidence of the sun trying to shine through the thick fog.

The initial inspiration for ‘Merlins in the Mist’ was, in fact, the view out of my caravan at one of the many Duxford air shows that I attend with my sales unit. Early morning mist shrouding the fabulous row of classic war birds sitting so peacefully waiting for the sun to break through, or, in this case, a row of wonderful war birds sitting so peacefully waiting for an enemy aircraft to come along and take them all out in one low level strafing run. I never could understand that! So many times one sees archive photographs of row after row of vulnerable aircraft on the ground ready to be taken out.

Spitfire QJ-L as shown, was a 616 Squadron RAF aircraft, but the QJ Squadron code letters were in fact shared with 92 Squadron RAF. This duplication has caused quite a lot of confusion and has generated interesting debate in recent years. QJ-L was flown by Flt Lt William Walker, born 1913, died 2012. He was, at the time of his death, the oldest surviving pilot of the Battle of Britain, and is sadly missed by everybody involved in aviation history.

Oil on Canvas

‘Preparing for action’

Supermarine Spitfire

This print depicts a Supermarine Spitfire Mk Vb of 303 (Polish) Squadron flown by the CO, Sqn Ldr J. Zumbach. A quick and efficient turnround of fighting aircraft on the front line was of paramount importance and the responsibility of the all-important ground crew.

The importance of the so-called “erks”, which included such duties as Armourers, Refuelers, Engine and Airframe Fitters etc, is often forgotten. Let us remember that, without these people, the aircraft would never have been able to take part in any action at all, and many were killed doing their duty on the ground. The image also helps to promote the fact that flying alongside the Spitfires were Hawker Hurricanes, as one is indeed landing in the background.

Part of the canvas was painted on site during the September 2005 Duxford airshow, with members of the public witnessing me painting out all the background trees to be replaced with the hedge. I found the trees overpowered the Spitfire airframe. I think the hedge helps the composition along by allowing the aircraft to overlap into the sky a bit. Note how the propeller sticks up above the horizon line, breaking up the straight line of the hedge. Removing the trees and replacing them with the hedge also allows that all-important view of the church that was requested in the commission brief.

I take a lot of interest in the skies and place a great deal of importance on them. The main subject in the composition is not the end of the story by any means. A lot of inexperienced artists put so much energy into painting the main subject that the rest of the painting is forgotten. I use this upper area of the canvas to enhance the illusion of depth and distance. You will notice how the cloud structure tightens up and the cloud ‘bottoms’ become narrower and thinner as they get close to the horizon. This only happens because they are further away, so there we have it….depth.

Oil on Canvas, in the collection of Dr Peter Stell

‘One to Remember’
Vickers-Armstrong VC10

The Vickers VC10 is a long-range British airliner designed and built by Vickers-Armstrongs Ltd. First flown at Brooklands, Surrey, in 1962, the airliner was specifically designed to operate from the shorter runways of the time. Its design characteristics allowed for excellent hot and high performance for operations from African airports, the painting opposite depicting a typical take off from Kenneth Kaunda International Airport, previously known as Lusaka International Airport in Zambia. The performance of the VC10 was such that it achieved the fastest crossing of the Atlantic by a jet airliner, a record still held to date for a sub-sonic airliner, flying the ocean in a little over 5 hours.

Although only a small number of VC10s were built, the type was operating with BOAC for many trouble free years to 1981.The VC10 was put to work within the RAF as a heavy lifter and airborne refuelling tanker aircraft. The type was retired from RAF service on 20 September 2013. It has been succeeded in the aerial refuelling tanker role by the Airbus Voyager. VC10 K3 ZA147 performed the final flight of the type on 25 September 2013.

My intention during the initial preparation of this commission, was to catch not only the beautiful lines of the VC10, but to portray it in a moody atmospheric environment that was to be part of the overall visual package. I do like to take advantage of such things as white livery, in this case the white top of the fuselage caught nicely against the dark stormy sky.

Interestingly, many people might think I have captured the aircraft flying down wind as opposed to into the wind as of course it should be. The rain columns in the background might give one the impression the wind is blowing from right to left, whereas in fact it is blowing from left to right. This effect is the result of a phenomenon known as wind shear effect. High level wind is blowing at a faster rate than lower levels due to land drag. This means the rain columns are distorted to the illustrated effect. The back lighting of the sun, illuminating the ground and aircraft, result in quite a common but dramatic effect.

Commissioned by, and hanging in the collection of Mr Simon Lind.

‘Foreign Fields’

Westland Lysander

The Lysander was designed as a short take off and landing aircraft, especially useful for the delivery of SOE (Special Operations Executive) agents deep in enemy territory. The Lysander was indeed the first aircraft to make use of fully automatic slats in the leading edge of the wings to aid the smooth flow of air as it passes over the wings at high angles of attack. This allowed for a much shorter take off and landing capability. Powered by the Bristol Mercury 850 h.p. XX radial engine, it was extremely quiet, and offered little pre-warning of its approach.

The painting depicts a 161 Squadron aircraft out of Tempsford, dropping into a French field near Puycelci - a long journey for a Lizzie! The painting was commissioned by Marc Hill, who owns a property very close to the area depicted in the painting. The light quality at night with a full moon is practically daylight in this region, and it was a delight to try and catch, with the moonlight reflecting off the upper surfaces of the wings.

I have introduced, with the approval of Marc, a little more immediate foreground detail to enhance the effect of depth in the canvas. This illusion can generate as much interest in a composition as the subject itself. I find this really satisfying, as it is all part of what constitutes a good painting ‘package’.

Oil on Canvas, in the collection of Mr Marc Hill

‘We Will Not Fail You’

Sea King HAR 3

The Royal Air Force ‘Search and Rescue Force’, or SAR Force, was the organisation responsible for the duty of aerial rescue around the United Kingdom until October 2015 when the responsibility was handed over to the civilian company Bristows.

The Sea King HAR3 entered RAF service in 1978. The aircraft in the search and rescue role were located at six sites around the UK, there being two aircraft at each location. The service operated around the clock 24 hrs a day. The machines and men were on standby with a 15-minute response time in daylight hours, and 45-minute response time in hours of darkness. The Sea King for its search role was fitted with advanced electronic equipment, ranging from homing equipment to satellite navigation systems, with advanced search radar and radio links.

For its rescue role, the aircraft is fitted out with a hydraulically operated lift winch, accompanied by an emergency electrically operated lift winch. An electrical generator is fitted to power up such items as cutting equipment etc.

This painting encompasses everything I love about my job. There is sea, moody sky and, of course, the inevitable aircraft, the beautiful Sea King. Yellow can be quite a tricky colour to handle in a painting, especially when it goes into a shaded area or a shadow is cast across it. It is very tempting to add just a touch of black to take the colour down, but this just makes it go green. Yes, yellow and black make green. I find red with a little burnt Sienna added takes the yellow down into shade nicely. I love painting the sea, the rougher the better. I served in the Royal Navy for several years and my favourite time would be bobbing up and down in the roughest seas.

This painting went on to win in 2014 ‘The Westland Helicopters Rotary Winged Flight Trophy’ at the Guild of Aviation Artists Annual Exhibition, held at the prestigious Mall Galleries in London.

Oil on Canvas, in the collection of the RAF Museum Hendon

‘Channel Dash’~ a Whirlwind encounter
Westland Whirlwind

It is a little known fact that the Westland Whirlwind was involved in the attack on the Scharnhorst during the Channel Dash. My painting depicts this event as a Whirlwind swoops low over the Battleship Scharnhorst chased by the ever-present Bf 109s. The Whirlwind was indeed a formidable attack aircraft, but unfortunately suffered engine problems throughout its short career, this being reflected in the fact that it was only taken on by two Squadrons, numbers 236 and 137. The engines, Rolls Royce Peregrines, suffered terribly from overheating problems.

The Whirlwind was, in many authoritative opinions, potentially one of the most deadly warbirds ever conceived, if it had been fitted out with the well-proven Rolls Royce Merlins. The image shows an aircraft from 137 Squadron.

The Whirlwind was the first aircraft to take advantage of the innovative cooling radiators embedded in the leading edges of the wings.

The last operational sortie flown by a Whirlwind was on 29th November 1943, after which they were replaced by Hawker Typhoons.

To me, an equally interesting element of the image is that of the Scharnhorst itself. One of several negative performance characteristics of the vessel was the fact that the bow and forward guns seemed to spend most of their time under water due to what is known as ‘Sympathetic Resonance’. This means that the natural rate at which the ship bobs up and down in the water is the same as the rate at which the ship encounters large waves, so the wave motion exacerbates the up and down motion of the ship. A modification to the bow was employed, known as an Atlantic Bow, which resulted in a longer bow section but it apparently had little effect. The ship bobbed up and down so much that the forward turrets were frequently out of action.

I would love to paint a pure WW11 marine scene involving a big Capital ship. It will certainly be done one day.

Reporters from ‘Fly Past’ magazine came to my studio to take photographs and interview me for a feature on the production of this painting.

Oil on Canvas

'Welcome to My World'

29 Sqn RAF 100th Anniversary

I was very proud to be commissioned by the Royal Air Force to paint a canvas for them to celebrate the 100th anniversary of 29 Squadron. The basis of the image was to reflect the changes the Squadron has experienced over the years. I tried to compose the canvas so as to offer a credible image that wasn't too far detached from reality. The basic initial concept was to have literally two paintings seamlessly joined together that expressed the progress of time and how it affected the Squadron.

I don't think it is a very good idea, from an art point of view, to try to depict all the aircraft types in the sky together occupying the same airspace. I think one feels the effect and impact of the time lapse more if the first and last aircraft are illustrated.

I thought it was rather a nice touch to have the position on the canvas where the two eras meet, i.e. in the middle, complemented by the bonding of two pilots (jet and WWI) chatting together as if it was just a normal thing.

Carol and I were invited as VIPs to attend the official unveiling of the painting at RAF Coningsby. We were sat with all the scrambled egg and smartly dressed people who obviously knew what they were talking about. We felt very posh. The climax of the day came when Prince William unveiled the painting. I got to shake hands with him and have a chat. He spoke about the painting with me, expressing an interest and knowledge. I was interviewed on camera by Kate Hemingway and featured on TV, completing a wonderful day.

Oil on Canvas, hanging in the Officers Mess at RAF Coningsby